Math

ISBN 978-0-7398-7036-5
ISBN 0-7398-7036-X

2003 Edition, Harcourt Achieve Inc.
Copyright © by Harcourt, Inc.

12 13 14 15 16 17 18 0982 16 15 14 13 12
4500348282

Rigby • Saxon • Steck-Vaughn

www.HarcourtAchieve.com
1.800.531.5015

Core Skills: Math
Grade 7
Table of Contents

Core Skills: Math, Grade 7, Table of Contents (cont.)

Core Skills: Math, Grade 7, Table of Contents (cont.)

Using Addition and Subtraction

Find the sum or difference.

1. 473
   +698

2. 720
   −486

3. 18.36
   + 5.28

4. 709.35
   − 40.74

5. 7.51 + 61.6

6. 63.2 − 0.25

7. 82.1 − 54.6

8. 30.3 + 4.99

9. 453 − 10.7

10. 0.9362 + 0.386

11. 721.7 + 5.08 + 5.2

12. 1.73 + 35 + 26.306

13. 12 + 5.928 + 6.6 + 14.072

14. 423.75 − 129.3 − 32 − 0.016

Mixed Applications

15. Unnex and Biron were once part of the country Nonlief. Nonlief then had an area of 36,200 square miles. After Unnex seceded, Nonlief had 28,560 square miles. Then Biron seceded, leaving Nonlief with 21,880 square miles. What are the areas of Unnex and Biron?

16. A total of $30 was placed in four envelopes, a different amount in each one. Money from the largest share was taken to double each of the other amounts. The resulting amounts were the same as before, but in different envelopes. What were the four amounts of money?

NUMBER SENSE

17. If 3 is the complement of 7, 98 is the complement of 2, and 845 is the complement of 155, what is the complement of 43?

Explain your answer.

Problem-Solving Strategy
Draw a Diagram

Draw a diagram on another piece of paper to solve each problem.

1. Mark, Wendy, Pilar, Christi, Lori, and Diego are lined up to receive awards. Wendy is fifth in line. Mark and Diego are between Lori and Wendy. Mark is three places in front of Christi. In what order are the students lined up?

_____

_____

2. In Angleton all streets run north and south or east and west. Tony lives 1 block west of Ramli and 3 blocks south of David. Paco lives 3 blocks west of Mike and 4 blocks north of Ed. If Mike lives 7 blocks north of Ramli, how many blocks apart do Ed and David live?

_____

Mixed Applications ▷ STRATEGIES
- Act It Out • Draw a Diagram
- Use Estimation • Write a Number Sentence

Choose a strategy and solve.

3. Eric won the 400-meter run in 1 minute 52 seconds. Chris would have won the race if she had cut 14 seconds from her time. How long did Chris take to run the race?

_____

4. Kevin can sign up for one sport and one other school activity. For a sport he can choose from soccer, basketball, football, tennis, and rowing. The other activities are choir, orchestra, or drama club. How many combinations of these activities are possible?

_____

MIXED REVIEW

Estimate the sum or difference.

1. $97.55 - 39.60$

_____

2. $812,344 - 187,675$

_____

3. $321.54 + 79.155$

_____

Find the sum or difference.

4. $71,429 + 36,802$

_____

5. $462.91 - 125.69$

_____

6. $622.79 + 876.28$

_____

Estimating Products and Quotients

Estimate each product by using front-end estimation. Then estimate each product by rounding.

1. 3.15
    $\times \quad 8$

2. 56.2
    $\times \quad 7$

3. 8.2
    $\times 1.5$

4. 7.11
    $\times \quad 88$

5. 12.6
    $\times 9.5$

6. 8.24
    $\times 5.4$

7. 40.27
    $\times \quad 7.8$

8. 79.6
    $\times 1.2$

Estimate each quotient by using compatible numbers.

9. $8.17 \div 1.9$

10. $36.15 \div 7.2$

11. $23.2 \div 6.4$

12. $55.9 \div 8.1$

13. $298.6 \div 2.22$

14. $102.75 \div 23.2$

15. $74.29 \div 2.86$

16. $714.3 \div 36.9$

17. $62,859.7 \div 15.25$

Mixed Applications

18. Craig is buying 2.76 pounds of cheese that is priced at $3.60 per pound. Estimate the cost as a range between two amounts.

19. Uncle Sid is spending $100 for a camera and some film. If he buys the camera for $67.95, about how many rolls of film can he buy at $4.90 each?

WRITER'S CORNER

20. Make up a multiplication problem in which the factors are both decimals and the product can be expressed as "a number between 8 and 15."

Using Multiplication

Place the decimal point in each product. Add zeros where necessary.

1.
```
   0.03
×     9
    2 7
```

2.
```
      1.5
×   0.2 5
    3 7 5
```

3.
```
   0.1 2 5
×    0.7 0
   8 7 5 0
```

4.
```
     3 0 0
×     1.8
   5 4 0 0
```

5.
```
   5 2.7 5
×      0.8
   4 2 2 0 0
```

6.
```
       3.88
×     5.43
   2 1 0 6 8 4
```

7.
```
     2.1 6 3
×   0.0 7 5
   1 6 2 2 2 5
```

8.
```
   0.0 8 7
×   0.5 6
   4 8 7 2
```

Find the product.

9.
```
   0.04
×     6
```

10.
```
    0.8
× 0.3
```

11.
```
   0.007
×      7
```

12.
```
   13.95
×    0.1
```

13.
```
    200
× 0.36
```

14.
```
     1.2
× 0.005
```

15.
```
   3.24
×   2.2
```

16.
```
      87
× 0.06
```

17.
```
   0.833
×    0.5
```

18.
```
   0.175
×   0.38
```

19.
```
    24.9
× 0.026
```

20.
```
   4.665
×    7.3
```

Mixed Applications

21. In 1960 the average speed of passenger aircraft within the U.S. was 235 miles per hour. By 1978 the average speed was 1.74 times that amount. To the nearest whole number, what was the average speed in 1978?

_____

22. Lauren and her sister can buy plane tickets to Los Angeles for $268 each. If they reserve seats three weeks in advance and fly on a weekend, each ticket would cost $155.75. Together, how much would they save at the lower rate? _____

LOGICAL REASONING

23. Check that $15,873 \times 7 = 111,111$. Now guess the missing numbers in these multiplication problems.

$15,873 \times 14 = $ _____ $15,873 \times 21 = $ _____ $15,873 \times$ ____ $= 888,888$

Check your guesses by multiplying.

4

Exploring Division
Decimal by a Decimal

Place the decimal point in the dividend so that the division problem is changed to a problem with a whole-number divisor. Write zeros if necessary.

1. $0.05\overline{)2.2765}$ $5\overline{)22765}$

2. $0.64\overline{)3.2}$ $64\overline{)32}$

3. $81.5\overline{)73.35}$ $815\overline{)7335}$

4. $0.072\overline{)417.6}$ $72\overline{)4176}$

Estimate. Then find the quotient.

5. $6.8\overline{)12.92}$

6. $2.6\overline{)33.8}$

7. $9.25\overline{)277.5}$

8. $2.24\overline{)2.688}$

9. $4.7\overline{)14.57}$

10. $9.1\overline{)65.52}$

11. $7.12\overline{)291.92}$

12. $3.03\overline{)36.966}$

13. $8.4\overline{)27.72}$

14. $2.3\overline{)158.7}$

15. $5.12\overline{)215.04}$

16. $3.61\overline{)324.9}$

17. $8.5\overline{)249.05}$

18. $0.7\overline{)107.8}$

19. $5.2\overline{)448.812}$

20. $6.4\overline{)210.56}$

Use the given division number sentence to help you predict the missing number. Use a calculator to check your predictions.

> Given: $345 \div 15 = 23$

21. $3.45 \div 0.15 =$ _____

22. $34.5 \div 1.5 =$ _____

23. $0.345 \div 0.015 =$ _____

24. $34.5 \div 0.15 =$ _____

25. $345 \div 1.5 =$ _____

26. $3.45 \div 15 =$ _____

27. $3.45 \div$ _____ $= 2.3$

28. _____ $\div 15 = 2.3$

LOGICAL REASONING

29. The value of the expression below is 1. Each digit from 1 through 9 is used only once. What are the two missing numbers?

$$1.23 + 0.08 - 0.67 + \underline{\hspace{2cm}} - \underline{\hspace{2cm}}$$

5

Using Division

Estimate. Then find the quotient.

1. $3\overline{)45.6}$

2. $8\overline{)25.52}$

3. $0.2\overline{)3}$

4. $0.5\overline{)303}$

5. $4.8\overline{)24.48}$

6. $0.03\overline{)1.575}$

7. $1.5\overline{)7.59}$

8. $0.012\overline{)0.816}$

Estimate. Then find the quotient, rounded to the place named.

nearest whole number: 9. $8.2\overline{)16.6}$ 10. $7\overline{)55.5}$ 11. $7.6\overline{)49.4}$

nearest tenth: 12. $7\overline{)37.9}$ 13. $0.44\overline{)1.26}$ 14. $9.6\overline{)64}$

nearest hundredth: 15. $3.2\overline{)6.9}$ 16. $0.18\overline{)0.59}$ 17. $0.47\overline{)4.527}$

nearest thousandth: 18. $6\overline{)11.8}$ 19. $5\overline{)2.424}$ 20. $13\overline{)20}$

Use the pattern to find the quotient.

21. $2{,}800 \div 8 = 350$
$280 \div 8 = 35$

$28.0 \div 8 =$ _____

$2.8 \div 8 =$ _____

22. $7{,}321 \div 0.5 = 14{,}642$
$732.1 \div 0.5 = 1{,}464.2$

$73.21 \div 0.5 =$ _____

$7.321 \div 0.5 =$ _____

Mixed Applications

23. The Leaning Tower of Pisa is a famous landmark in Italy. Each year it tilts a little farther. During this century the tilt at the top has increased by about 1.1 millimeters per year. At this rate, by how much would the tilt increase in 15 years?

_____

24. About 800,000 tourists bought tickets to visit the Leaning Tower of Pisa one year. This brought the city about $2 million from ticket sales. Use these figures to estimate the price of one ticket.

_____

NUMBER SENSE

25. You can make up a number pattern with whole numbers and decimals. What are the missing numbers?

_____ , 40, _____ , 1.6,   0.32,   0.064,   0.0128

6

Problem-Solving Strategy
Guess and Check

1. Jerry was 6 years old when his mother was 30. Now she is twice his age. How old is Jerry?

_____

2. Moira bought $0.65 worth of stamps. She paid for them with 15 coins. What coins did she use?

_____

Mixed Applications ➔ **STRATEGIES**
- Draw a Diagram • Guess and Check
- Write a Number Sentence • Use Estimation

Choose a strategy and solve.

3. An office building has 10 floors of the same height. How many times as far from the ground is the ninth floor than the third floor?

_____

4. The difference between twice a number and half the number is 30. What is the number?

_____

5. Lisa sold costume jewelry at a bazaar. The first hour she sold 2 bracelets and 3 rings for a total of $26. Later a customer bought 2 rings and paid $12. All bracelets were priced the same. All rings were priced the same. How much did a bracelet cost?

_____

6. Tara wants to weigh her three stuffed animals. They will only fit on the scale two at a time. Together Addie and Blissy weigh 18 ounces, Blissy and Corky weigh 22 ounces, and Addie and Corky weigh 12 ounces. How much does each animal weigh?

_____

NUMBER SENSE

7. Use any of the digits 1, 3, and 9 and the operation signs + and/or − to write all the whole numbers from 1 through 13. Each digit can be used only once in each expression.

Examples:

Number	Expression
1	1
2	3 − 1

_____

_____

_____

Powers and Exponents

Write in exponent form.

1. five squared

_____

2. eight to the 5th power

_____

3. nine cubed

_____

4. $2 \times 2 \times 2 \times 2$

_____

5. $7 \times 7 \times 7 \times 7 \times 7 \times 7$

_____

6. 2.3×2.3

_____

Find the value.

7. 5^4

_____

8. thirteen squared

_____

9. $(1.2)^2$

_____

10. 18^0

_____

11. one thousand squared

_____

12. $7^2 \times 7^0$

_____

Mixed Applications

13. Mai bought a new car. She drove 6^3 miles the first month and 6^4 miles the second month. How much farther did she drive the second month?

_____

14. Mai bought gasoline at $1.39 per gallon. She paid $20.85. How many gallons did she buy?

_____

MIXED REVIEW

Estimate the product or quotient.

1. 23.9×4.3

_____

2. $73.1 \div 9.2$

_____

3. 6×19.98

_____

4. $289.3 \div 7.25$

_____

Find the product or quotient.

5. $3,052 \times 44$

_____

6. $5,280 \div 30$

_____

7. 6.9×1.5

_____

8. $90 \div 1.2$

_____

Data Collection

Oaksford Middle School surveyed a sample of 100 students. The students were asked which assembly program they liked best during the year. The results of the survey are tallied at the right. When you make predictions, assume that the sample in the survey was unbiased.

Oaksford Middle School Survey Results		
Favorite Program	Students	
	Tally	Number
Sing-Along	||||| ||||| ||||| ||||| ||||| |||||	30
Puppet Show	||||| ||||| |||||		
Story Theater Group	||||| ||||| ||||| |||||		
Magic Show	||||| ||||| ||||| ||||| ||||| ||||| ||||| |||		

1. Complete the number column in the table.

2. Suppose Oaksford Middle School has 612 students. Predict how many of them liked the Story Theater Group best.

   _____

3. Of the 612 students, predict how many of them liked the Magic Show best.

   _____

4. Predict how many more of the 612 students liked the Magic Show better than the Sing-Along.

   _____

Mixed Applications

5. A school has 789 students. In a random sample of 50 students, 6 make the same choice as you. Predict how many in the school would make this choice.

   _____

6. Tickets to a school play cost $1.50 for a student and $2.50 for an adult. Clara sold 5 tickets for a total of $10.50. How many of these were student tickets?

   _____

VISUAL THINKING

7. Start with the top letter and move down to the left or right, one letter at a time. How many ways can you spell *SHOW*? (One path is shown for you.)

   _____

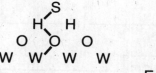

8. How many ways can you spell *DANCE*?

   _____

Problem-Solving Strategy
Use a Table

The table shows how public lands in the United States were used
for some types of recreation in the years 1983 through 1987.
Use it to answer Exercises 1 and 2.

1. In which years were about
   3,000,000 visitor hours
   spent on winter sports?

   _____

2. In 1983 about 17,000,000
   visitor hours were spent on
   boating. To the nearest
   million, about how many hours
   were spent on fishing?

   _____

Visitor Hours for Public Lands (in thousands)			
Year	Camping and Hunting	Fishing and Boating	Winter Sports
1983	177,040	37,159	2,917
1984	146,930	25,447	2,894
1985	117,239	25,964	5,023
1986	130,766	34,118	6,025
1987	252,939	38,072	3,259

Use the graph for Exercises 3–5.

3. From the graph, find the year in which people
   spent about $2,500,000,000 going to the movies.

   _____

4. In which year did they spend about 1.1 billion

   dollars? _____

5. The increase in money spent on tickets from 1960 to
   1978 could mean that going to the movies became
   more popular. What else could this increase mean?

   _____

   _____

Year	Movie Ticket Sales
1960	$1,000,000,000
1965	$1,100,000,000
1970	$1,500,000,000
1975	$2,500,000,000
1978	$4,300,000,000

NUMBER SENSE

6. Look for a pattern. Complete the last number.

   3.6 million; 1,800 thousand; 9 hundred thousand; 450 thousand; _____ thousand

Line Graphs

Use the graph for yogurt sales
for Exercises 1–3 and 6.

1. In which month were sales first

   over $150? _____

2. What month showed sales of

   $375? _____

3. What month showed the greatest

   increase in sales? _____

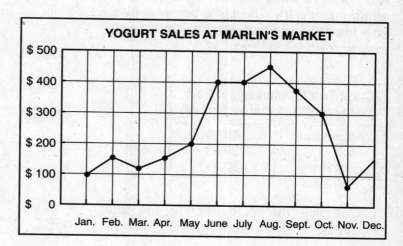

4. Draw a line graph to show the number of
   movies rented in a video rental store.
   Use the data given.

Video Rentals					
Year	1986	1987	1988	1989	1990
Videos Rented	1,000	1,500	3,000	2,800	3,500

5. In which year did sales drop from the

   previous year? _____

Mixed Applications

6. In general, during what part of the year
   does Marlin's sell the most yogurt?

   _____

7. Write the total number of video rentals
   from 1986 through 1990 in scientific
   notation.

   _____

LOGICAL REASONING

8. If $\triangle\square + \square\triangle = 77$ and $\square - \triangle = 3$, what digits do the $\triangle$ and
   $\square$ represent?

   $\triangle$ = _____ ; $\square$ = _____

Circle Graphs

Kam Shing's class is planning a trip to an amusement park. The table below shows how the students budgeted the money they earned for the trip.

Class Trip to Amusement Park (Budget for Each Dollar Earned)	
Admissions	$0.60
Food	$0.25
Souvenirs	$0.15

1. Complete the circle graph for the data in the table.

2. If the students earned $420 for the trip, how much can they plan to spend for

   admissions? _____   food? _____

   souvenirs? _____

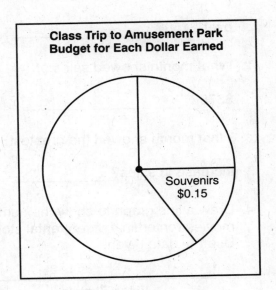

Class Trip to Amusement Park Budget for Each Dollar Earned

Souvenirs $0.15

Mixed Applications

During a school carnival, students from Lewiston Middle School raised funds by selling crafts and food and from ticket sales for games and for a school play. Of each dollar earned, $0.15 came from games, while craft sales brought in 3 times as much. Food sales, $0.32, were 4 times the income from the play.

3. Complete the circle graph. Show the amounts per dollar earned from craft sales and the play.

Lewiston Middle School Carnival Source of Each Dollar Earned

Craft Sales

Games $0.15

Food Sales $0.32

School Play

MIXED REVIEW

Write in exponent form. Then find the value.

1. $4 \times 4 \times 4$

2. eleven squared

3. 5 cubed

4. $0.7 \times 0.7 \times 4^0$

_____   _____   _____   _____

12

Different Graphs, Same Data

The *Littleton Weekly* published these high and low temperatures for the previous week. Use the table of temperatures to solve Exercises 1–5.

Temperatures (degrees Fahrenheit)							
	Mon.	Tues.	Wed.	Thurs.	Fri.	Sat.	Sun.
High	82°	85°	77°	68°	75°	70°	84°
Low	58°	60°	62°	50°	48°	52°	56°

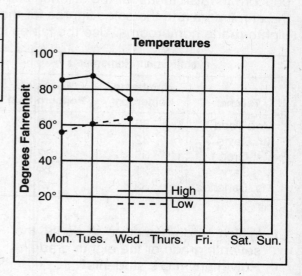

1. Complete the double-line graph at the right for the temperatures.

2. Which day had the least change in

   temperature? _____

3. Which two consecutive days showed a drop in

   the high temperature? _____

Mixed Applications

4. Complete the double-bar graph below for the temperatures.

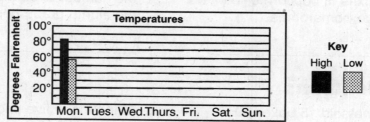

5. Which graph do you think gives a better picture of the temperature differences, the double-line graph or the double-bar graph?

   _____

   _____

NUMBER SENSE

6. If $5^3 - 5^2 = \triangle^2$ and $3^3 + 3^2 = \square^2$,

   what is the value of $\triangle^\square$? _____

Central Tendency
Mean, Median, Mode

Students at the Everett Middle School are selling boxes of popcorn to raise funds for the science center. The tables show the enrollment and the sales figures for the seventh- and eighth-grade homerooms. Use the tables for Exercises 1–4.

Seventh-Grade Homerooms		
Teacher	Number in Homeroom	Boxes of Popcorn Sold
Mrs. Todd	30	12
Mr. Davis	32	25
Ms. Green	35	32
Mr. Gary	31	24
Ms. Sanchez	32	12

Eighth-Grade Homerooms		
Teacher	Number in Homeroom	Boxes of Popcorn Sold
Mr. Han	33	8
Ms. Gibson	36	28
Mrs. Majia	35	40
Mr. Ray	36	36

1. Which grade has more students, the seventh grade or the eighth grade? How many more students?

_____

2. In which grade is the mean number of students per homeroom greater, the seventh or the eighth grade? How much greater?

_____

3. Find the mean, mode, and median of the number of boxes of popcorn sold in the seventh-grade homerooms.

_____

4. Find the mean, mode, and median of the number of boxes of popcorn sold in the eighth-grade homerooms.

_____

Mixed Applications

5. In three days Gina sold 15 boxes. On the second day, she sold 1 more than on the first. On the third day, she sold 5 more than on the first. How many boxes did she sell the third day?

_____

6. Mario made five phone calls lasting 4, 6, 8, 15, and 21 minutes. After another call, the median length of the phone calls was 10 minutes. What was the mean length of the six calls?

_____

LOGICAL REASONING

7. Only one girl is telling the truth.

Eve: "Doris and I are twins."
Ann: "Doris and Eve are not twins."
Doris: "Ann and I are not twins."

Who are the twins? _____

Exploring Divisibility

Is the number divisible by 4? Write *yes* or *no*.

1. 900   2. 3,000   3. 2,050   4. 7,512   5. 15,028

_____   _____   _____   _____   _____

Tell whether the number is divisible by 2, 3, 4, or 6.

6. 44   7. 38   8. 726   9. 2,112   10. 1,221

_____   _____   _____   _____   _____

Tell whether the number is divisible by 2, 3, 4, or 9.

11. 207   12. 126   13. 732   14. 4,104   15. 1,992

_____   _____   _____   _____   _____

16. Find four numbers that are divisible by both 4 and 9.

_____

17. Find four numbers that are divisible by 2, 3, and 5.

_____

18. Find four numbers that are divisible by both 4 and 6.

_____

19. Find four numbers that are divisible by both 2 and 9.

_____

Miguel has 225 baseball cards. He plans to keep 75 cards and give the rest to his friends.

20. Can Miguel give an equal number of cards to 6 friends? Explain. _____

_____

21. Can Miguel give an equal number of cards to 4 friends? Explain. _____

_____

NUMBER SENSE

A number is divided by 2, and the remainder is 1. The same number is divided by 3, and the remainder is 2.

22. Find the smallest such number. _____

23. Find the next larger number. _____

Factors, Primes, and Composites

List all the factors of each number.

1. 6

   _____

2. 35

   _____

3. 19

   _____

4. 39

   _____

5. 44

   _____

   _____

6. 64

   _____

   _____

7. 56

   _____

   _____

8. 80

   _____

   _____

Identify each number as *prime* or *composite*.

9. 18 _____

10. 3 _____

11. 19 _____

12. 102 _____

13. 41 _____

14. 63 _____

15. 11 _____

16. 51 _____

Mixed Applications

17. Cheryl brought 30 muffins to a party. List all the ways she can arrange them on a platter in equal rows.

    _____

    _____

    _____

18. Donya is setting up tables for 24 people at the party. The same number of people will sit at each table, and no one will sit alone. How many people can sit at each table? List all possibilities.

    _____

WRITER'S CORNER

19. Write a problem similar to Exercise 17 or Exercise 18. Use the facts that you know about divisibility.

    _____

    _____

    _____

    _____

Prime Factorization

1. Complete the factor mobile.

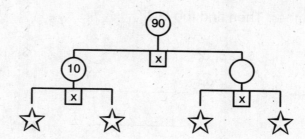

Draw a factor tree to show the prime factorization of each number. Then use exponents to write each prime factorization.

2. 36

3. 51

4. 32

5. 75

_____   _____   _____   _____

Write the composite number for each prime factorization. You may wish to use a calculator.

6. $2^2 \times 3 \times 5^2$ _____

7. $2 \times 3^2 \times 7$ _____

8. $3^3 \times 5$ _____

9. 2×5^3 _____

Mixed Applications

10. Find all the numbers with prime factors 2, 3, and 7 that are less than 200.

_____

11. If a number is divisible by 4 and 7, the number must have at least six factors. What are they?

_____

NUMBER SENSE

12. What number comes next? 4, 9, 25, 49, 121, _____ Explain the pattern.

_____

_____

Greatest Common Factor

List the factors of each number. Then find the GCF.

1. 18, 27

18: _____

27: _____

GCF: _____

2. 28, 35

28: _____

35: _____

GCF: _____

3. 12, 15

12: _____

15: _____

GCF: _____

Use prime factorization to find the GCF.

4. 15, 35

15: _____

35: _____

GCF: _____

5. 24, 36

24: _____

36: _____

GCF: _____

6. 21, 45

21: _____

45: _____

GCF: _____

Mixed Applications

Forest City has ordered 36 maple trees and 54 dogwood trees to be planted in groups in a city park. Each group will have the same number of maple trees and dogwood trees.

7. Can the trees be planted in

6 groups? _____

8 groups? _____

9 groups? _____

8. What is the greatest number of groups of trees that can be planted? How many trees of each kind would be in

one group? _____

_____

NUMBER SENSE

Find the missing numbers. Explain the pattern.

9. 1, 3, ___, 15, 25, 75

10. 1, 2, 7, ___, 49, 98

11. 1, 2, 4, 5, 10, 20, 25, ___, 100

12. 1, 2, 3, 4, 6, 8, 12, ___, 24, 48

_____

Equivalent Fractions and Simplest Form

Write an equivalent fraction for each.

1. $\frac{3}{4}$ _____

2. $\frac{1}{7}$ _____

3. $\frac{4}{9}$ _____

4. $\frac{16}{20}$ _____

5. $\frac{24}{42}$ _____

Write in simplest form.

6. $\frac{7}{42}$ _____

7. $\frac{2}{18}$ _____

8. $\frac{6}{10}$ _____

9. $\frac{2}{16}$ _____

10. $\frac{75}{100}$ _____

11. $\frac{4}{32}$ _____

12. $\frac{3}{12}$ _____

13. $\frac{21}{28}$ _____

14. $\frac{15}{27}$ _____

15. $\frac{5}{20}$ _____

16. $\frac{6}{15}$ _____

17. $\frac{14}{49}$ _____

18. $\frac{30}{36}$ _____

19. $\frac{35}{50}$ _____

20. $\frac{12}{36}$ _____

21. $\frac{48}{54}$ _____

22. $\frac{15}{60}$ _____

23. $\frac{32}{64}$ _____

24. $\frac{30}{270}$ _____

25. $\frac{28}{77}$ _____

Mixed Applications

26. Calvin hiked 18 miles in 6 hours. If he continues at the same pace, how much farther can he hike in the next 2 hours?

27. Hamako made 4 hits in 9 times at bat. If she keeps the same success level, how many hits should she make in 18 times at bat?

28. In how many ways can 18 hikers be organized into 2 or more groups for trail clearing if all groups have the same number of hikers?

MIXED REVIEW

Tell whether each number is divisible by 2, 3, 4, 5, 6, 9, or 10.

1. 12

2. 30

3. 360

4. 96

For the set of numbers 7, 6, 11, 16, 9, and 11, find each measure.

5. mean _____

6. mode _____

7. median _____

8. range _____

Problem-Solving Strategy
Find a Pattern

1. In Tara's math class, each student made up a number pattern for classmates to identify. These are the numbers that Tara wrote. When you find the pattern, write the first and seventh numbers in the table.

Tara's Pattern						
1st	2nd	3rd	4th	5th	6th	7th
	$\frac{3}{8}$	$\frac{5}{16}$	$\frac{9}{32}$	$\frac{17}{64}$	$\frac{33}{128}$	

2. In 1990 first-class mail cost $0.25 for the first ounce or fraction, and $0.20 for each additional ounce or fraction. Adrianne sent two letters. One weighed 3 ounces. The other weighed $5\frac{1}{2}$ ounces. What was the total cost?

_____

3. Derrick told Sue, "Write three two-digit numbers. I'll add three more and give you the sum right away." Sue wrote 53, 42, and 31. Then Derrick wrote 46, 57, and 68 and said the sum was 297. Was he right? What pattern did he use?

_____

_____

Mixed Applications → **STRATEGIES**
- Draw a Diagram • Guess and Check
- Find a Pattern • Use a Table or Graph

Choose a strategy and solve.

4. When Felix started his paper route, he had 25 customers. Every second week he gained 2 new customers. Every third week he lost a customer. How many customers did he have in the seventh week?

_____

5. In three days Speedy the squirrel ate 30 peanuts. On both the second and third day, Speedy ate 7 peanuts more than on the day before. How many peanuts did Speedy eat the first day?

_____

VISUAL THINKING

6. How many squares are in this

figure? _____

How many triangles? _____

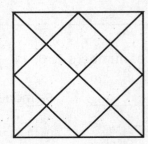

Comparing Fractions

Rewrite each pair of fractions using the LCD.

1. $\frac{2}{5}, \frac{1}{6}$ _____

2. $\frac{2}{3}, \frac{4}{5}$ _____

3. $\frac{3}{4}, \frac{3}{8}$ _____

4. $\frac{1}{8}, \frac{3}{7}$ _____

5. $\frac{5}{6}, \frac{1}{2}$ _____

6. $\frac{3}{11}, \frac{1}{7}$ _____

7. $\frac{2}{3}, \frac{7}{10}$ _____

8. $\frac{1}{4}, \frac{4}{5}$ _____

9. $\frac{5}{8}, \frac{3}{5}$ _____

10. $\frac{1}{3}, \frac{2}{7}$ _____

11. $\frac{3}{10}, \frac{2}{9}$ _____

12. $\frac{5}{7}, \frac{3}{4}$ _____

Compare. Write $<$, $>$, or $=$.

13. $\frac{1}{5} \bigcirc \frac{1}{4}$

14. $\frac{1}{6} \bigcirc \frac{2}{7}$

15. $\frac{4}{5} \bigcirc \frac{7}{10}$

16. $\frac{3}{11} \bigcirc \frac{3}{7}$

17. $\frac{5}{8} \bigcirc \frac{3}{5}$

18. $\frac{1}{3} \bigcirc \frac{3}{8}$

19. $\frac{3}{9} \bigcirc \frac{4}{12}$

20. $\frac{3}{8} \bigcirc \frac{5}{7}$

21. $\frac{2}{3} \bigcirc \frac{3}{9}$

22. $\frac{5}{8} \bigcirc \frac{4}{9}$

23. $\frac{4}{7} \bigcirc \frac{3}{5}$

24. $\frac{4}{6} \bigcirc \frac{8}{12}$

Mixed Applications

25. Shumarra exercises four dogs — Bing, Muskie, Cowboy, and Teddy. Teddy is 5 pounds heavier than Muskie. Cowboy is 8 pounds lighter than Bing, who is twice as heavy as Muskie. If Teddy weighs 25 pounds, what does each of the other dogs weigh?

   _____

26. Cramer's Market and Buyrite usually sell Vitalin pet food at the same price. This week Cramer's Market advertises Vitalin pet food at $\frac{1}{8}$ off, while Buyrite advertises it at $\frac{1}{10}$ off. Which store has the better buy?

   _____

NUMBER SENSE

You can write $\frac{8}{25}$ as $\frac{2^3}{5^2}$.

For each fraction, use exponents in the numerator and denominator to write an equivalent fraction.

27. $\frac{4}{9}$ _____

28. $\frac{4}{27}$ _____

29. $\frac{36}{49}$ _____

30. $\frac{81}{125}$ _____

31. $\frac{9}{32}$ _____

Ordering Fractions

Rewrite each group of fractions using the LCD.

1. $\frac{2}{5}, \frac{1}{3}, \frac{3}{15}$ _____

2. $\frac{1}{6}, \frac{3}{5}, \frac{2}{3}$ _____

3. $\frac{2}{5}, \frac{1}{2}, \frac{5}{8}$ _____

4. $\frac{3}{4}, \frac{1}{3}, \frac{1}{2}$ _____

5. $\frac{1}{5}, \frac{1}{2}, \frac{2}{3}$ _____

6. $\frac{3}{5}, \frac{7}{10}, \frac{1}{4}$ _____

Order from least to greatest.

7. $\frac{1}{2}, \frac{1}{3}, \frac{2}{5}$ _____

8. $\frac{5}{6}, \frac{7}{12}, \frac{2}{3}$ _____

9. $\frac{2}{7}, \frac{2}{5}, \frac{3}{10}$ _____

10. $\frac{2}{5}, \frac{5}{6}, \frac{2}{3}$ _____

11. $\frac{1}{2}, \frac{3}{10}, \frac{4}{9}$ _____

12. $\frac{2}{3}, \frac{5}{6}, \frac{3}{4}$ _____

Mixed Applications

13. Carol, Lennie, and Brian went skating around the pond. They started out from the dock. Carol skated around the pond once every 6 minutes. It took Lennie 4 minutes and Brian 8 minutes. How many minutes did it take before all three passed by the dock at the same time?

_____

14. Price's Pet Store had twice as many dogs as cats. Some customers bought 6 of the dogs. Then there were twice as many cats as dogs. How many cats and dogs were there at the beginning?

_____

NUMBER SENSE

15. In the subtraction problems below, notice that each problem has two numbers whose digits are in reverse order. Find the differences.

$$725 - 527$$ $$83 - 38$$ $$531 - 135$$

Make up three of your own subtraction problems. Choose a number, reverse the digits, and write the lesser number under the greater one.

_____ _____ _____

What do all six answers have in common? Look for common

factors. _____

Problem-Solving Strategy
Draw a Diagram

1. Inés and Diane are jogging back and forth along a one-mile path. They started out at 9:00 A.M. from opposite ends of the path. They passed each other in 10 minutes, when Inés had gone $\frac{1}{3}$ mile. At what time will they first meet at one end of the path? Assume they keep jogging at the same rates.

   _____

2. A spider rested on a wall 5 feet from the floor. It starts climbing up the wall, $\frac{1}{2}$ foot every hour. When it reaches a height of 8 feet, it starts climbing back down, $\frac{1}{2}$ foot every hour. How high up the wall will the spider be at the end of 10 hours?

   _____

Mixed Applications ▶ STRATEGIES
- Draw a Diagram • Guess and Check
- Find a Pattern • Use a Table or Graph

Choose a strategy and solve.

3. Drake's Apparel advertised a clothing sale. The first day, all clothing was marked $\frac{1}{4}$ off. The second day, unsold items were marked $\frac{2}{5}$ off; the third day, $\frac{3}{6}$ (or $\frac{1}{2}$) off, and so on. If the markdowns continued this way, on which day were prices marked $\frac{3}{4}$ off?

   _____

4. On the east side of Holly Hill, you climb 2 feet higher for every 11 yards you climb toward the west. If you climb the hill to a height of 12 feet, how far west have you moved from the foot of the hill?

   _____

MIXED REVIEW

Identify each number as *prime* or *composite*. Then list all the factors.

1. 2 _____

2. 37 _____

3. 27 _____

4. 54 _____

5. 19 _____

6. 63 _____

Estimating Sums and Differences

Estimate the sum or difference by rounding to the nearest half.

1. $\begin{array}{r} \frac{7}{8} \\ + \frac{15}{16} \\ \hline \end{array}$

2. $\begin{array}{r} 3\frac{5}{6} \\ + \frac{8}{9} \\ \hline \end{array}$

3. $\begin{array}{r} 1\frac{1}{2} \\ - \frac{7}{12} \\ \hline \end{array}$

4. $\begin{array}{r} 4\frac{8}{9} \\ - \frac{5}{6} \\ \hline \end{array}$

5. $\begin{array}{r} 6\frac{1}{8} \\ + 1\frac{2}{5} \\ \hline \end{array}$

6. $\begin{array}{r} 8\frac{1}{3} \\ - \frac{9}{10} \\ \hline \end{array}$

7. $\begin{array}{r} 6\frac{5}{6} \\ - \frac{8}{9} \\ \hline \end{array}$

8. $\begin{array}{r} 6\frac{1}{9} \\ - 5\frac{9}{10} \\ \hline \end{array}$

9. $\begin{array}{r} 1\frac{1}{8} \\ + 1\frac{5}{6} \\ \hline \end{array}$

10. $\begin{array}{r} 2\frac{4}{5} \\ + 4\frac{7}{8} \\ \hline \end{array}$

11. $\begin{array}{r} 3\frac{3}{7} \\ + 8\frac{1}{2} \\ \hline \end{array}$

12. $\begin{array}{r} 15\frac{3}{5} \\ - 5\frac{2}{3} \\ \hline \end{array}$

13. $\begin{array}{r} 5\frac{5}{8} \\ - 4\frac{1}{6} \\ \hline \end{array}$

14. $\begin{array}{r} 8\frac{3}{7} \\ + 5\frac{1}{6} \\ \hline \end{array}$

15. $\begin{array}{r} \frac{1}{8} \\ + 4\frac{9}{16} \\ \hline \end{array}$

Mixed Applications

16. Which fraction does not belong? Explain. $\frac{3}{5}, \frac{5}{6}, \frac{3}{7}, \frac{5}{8}, \frac{5}{9}$

_____

_____

17. Kelly mailed packages weighing $\frac{3}{8}$ pound, $5\frac{1}{2}$ pounds, and $3\frac{1}{16}$ pounds. Estimate the total weight of the packages.

_____

18. Rick bicycled $\frac{7}{8}$ mile to the post office. From there he bicycled $\frac{3}{5}$ mile to the park, where he rode another $\frac{1}{2}$ mile. He then bicycled $\frac{7}{10}$ mile home. About how many miles did he bicycle?

_____

NUMBER SENSE

The fraction $\frac{1+2+3+4+5+6}{7+8+9}$ is equivalent to $\frac{21}{24}$, or $\frac{7}{8}$.

Write an equivalent fraction using the digits 1 through 9 once.

19. $\frac{1}{4}$ _____

20. $\frac{1}{2}$ _____

Adding and Subtracting Fractions

Estimate. Then find the exact sum or difference. Write the answer in simplest form.

1. $\dfrac{1}{3}$
    $+\dfrac{1}{9}$

2. $\dfrac{1}{4}$
    $+\dfrac{7}{8}$

3. $\dfrac{5}{8}$
    $-\dfrac{1}{2}$

4. $\dfrac{2}{3}$
    $-\dfrac{1}{6}$

5. $\dfrac{1}{3}$
    $+\dfrac{7}{12}$

6. $\dfrac{1}{2}$
    $+\dfrac{4}{5}$

7. $\dfrac{5}{6}$
    $-\dfrac{3}{4}$

8. $\dfrac{3}{4}$
    $+\dfrac{5}{6}$

9. $\dfrac{5}{6}$
    $-\dfrac{3}{8}$

10. $\dfrac{4}{5}$
    $+\dfrac{11}{20}$

11. $\dfrac{2}{3} + \dfrac{1}{6} + \dfrac{1}{4}$ _____

12. $\dfrac{1}{2} + \dfrac{5}{6} + \dfrac{3}{8}$ _____

13. $\dfrac{19}{25} - \dfrac{3}{5}$ _____

Mixed Applications

14. Althea spent $\frac{3}{4}$ of her earnings last month. She spent $\frac{1}{4}$ on recreation, $\frac{1}{6}$ on art supplies, and the rest on clothes. What part of her earnings did she spend on clothes?

_____

15. The library has enough videocassettes to display equal numbers of them in groups of 3, 5, or 9. What is the least number of videocassettes the library can have?

_____

LOGICAL REASONING

Fill in the missing numerators.

16. The fractions have a sum of 1. The numerators have a sum of 4.

$$\dfrac{\boxed{}}{2} + \dfrac{\boxed{}}{5} + \dfrac{\boxed{}}{10} = 1$$

17. The fractions have a sum of 1. The numerators have a sum of 5.

$$\dfrac{\boxed{}}{2} + \dfrac{\boxed{}}{5} + \dfrac{\boxed{}}{10} = 1$$

18. The fractions have a sum of 1. The numerators have a sum of 9.

$$\dfrac{\boxed{}}{4} + \dfrac{\boxed{}}{6} + \dfrac{\boxed{}}{12} = 1$$

19. The fractions have a sum of 1. The numerators have a sum of 5.

$$\dfrac{\boxed{}}{4} + \dfrac{\boxed{}}{6} + \dfrac{\boxed{}}{12} = 1$$

Adding Mixed Numbers

Find the sum. Write the answer in simplest form.

1. $9\frac{1}{2}$
    $+1\frac{1}{2}$

2. 5
    $+3\frac{1}{3}$

3. $2\frac{4}{5}$
    $+16\frac{2}{5}$

4. $7\frac{1}{2}$
    $+2\frac{1}{4}$

5. $8\frac{5}{6}$
    $+3\frac{2}{3}$

6. $9\frac{3}{4}$
    $+15\frac{1}{2}$

7. $5\frac{1}{12}$
    $+2\frac{3}{4}$

8. $21\frac{1}{6}$
    $+4\frac{1}{8}$

9. $2\frac{1}{2}$
    $+7\frac{5}{6}$

10. $3\frac{7}{10}$
    $+9\frac{1}{6}$

11. $16\frac{3}{4}$
    $+5\frac{2}{3}$

12. $15\frac{1}{8}$
    $+6\frac{1}{10}$

13. $6\frac{3}{4}$
    $+\frac{5}{6}$

14. $8\frac{4}{5}$
    $+1\frac{3}{8}$

15. $10\frac{1}{7}$
    $+4\frac{3}{5}$

16. $2\frac{7}{8} + 3\frac{1}{2} + 5 + 3\frac{1}{4}$ _____

17. $5\frac{1}{2} + 2\frac{1}{3} + 9\frac{1}{6} + 2$ _____

18. $5\frac{1}{4} + 3\frac{1}{12} + 6 + 4\frac{1}{6}$ _____

19. $2\frac{1}{15} + 7\frac{2}{5} + 4 + 3\frac{1}{3}$ _____

Mixed Applications

20. Four friends spent an hour picking strawberries. Jennifer picked $1\frac{5}{6}$ quarts, Ilia picked $1\frac{3}{4}$ quarts, Lee picked $1\frac{1}{2}$ quarts, and Wendy picked $2\frac{1}{8}$ quarts. How many quarts did they pick?

    _____

21. Five sections of fencing around a garden are 7 yards long, $8\frac{3}{4}$ yards long, $12\frac{1}{2}$ yards long, $15\frac{1}{3}$ yards long, and $7\frac{3}{4}$ yards long. What is the total length of the fencing?

    _____

NUMBER SENSE

Use the numbers in the box for Exercises 22–23.

$\frac{1}{8}$	$\frac{1}{6}$	$\frac{1}{4}$	$\frac{1}{3}$	$\frac{1}{2}$	$1\frac{1}{8}$

22. Find three different numbers whose sum is 1. _____

23. Find three different numbers whose sum is $\frac{3}{4}$. _____

Subtracting Mixed Numbers

Find the difference. Write the answer in simplest form.

1. $18\frac{1}{3}$
   -12

2. $17\frac{3}{5}$
   $-\;6\frac{1}{5}$

3. $9\frac{5}{8}$
   $-7\frac{1}{8}$

4. $11\frac{5}{9}$
   $-\;3\frac{2}{9}$

5. $17\frac{3}{4}$
   $-10\frac{1}{8}$

6. $12\frac{5}{6}$
   $-\;5\frac{2}{3}$

7. $24\frac{3}{5}$
   $-11\frac{3}{10}$

8. $16\frac{3}{4}$
   $-\;8\frac{5}{16}$

9. $10\frac{11}{12}$
   $-\;6\frac{1}{4}$

10. $9\frac{7}{8}$
    $-6\frac{13}{24}$

11. 7
    $-5\frac{1}{6}$

12. 16
    $-\;7\frac{3}{8}$

13. $22\frac{1}{6}$
    $-15\frac{2}{3}$

14. $10\frac{1}{8}$
    $-\;9\frac{3}{4}$

15. $4\frac{3}{10}$
    $-1\frac{4}{5}$

16. $15 - 3\frac{5}{6}$ _____

17. $6\frac{3}{8} - 5\frac{5}{8}$ _____

18. $9\frac{3}{10} - 5\frac{3}{5}$ _____

Mixed Applications

19. Dana spent 3 hours baby-sitting for a neighbor. She and the children played games for $1\frac{3}{4}$ hours and watched TV for $\frac{1}{2}$ hour. The rest of the time, Dana read stories. How much time did Dana spend reading stories?

_____

20. Quincy went to see two one-act plays. With an intermission of $\frac{1}{6}$ hour, the evening lasted $2\frac{1}{2}$ hours. The first play was $1\frac{1}{4}$ hours long. How long did the second play last?

_____

VISUAL THINKING

21. Draw 12 squares by connecting dots in the figure at the right.

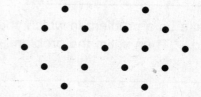

Problem-Solving Strategy
Solve a Simpler Problem

1. There are 8 students playing badminton. Each student is paired with each of the other students to play one game. How many games will the students play?

_____

2. At Lu's school, 5 students are trying out for the chorus. Only 3 students are needed. In how many ways can 3 students be chosen from the 5?

_____

Mixed Applications	→	STRATEGIES	• Draw a Diagram • Solve a Simpler Problem
			• Guess and Check • Use a Table or Diagram

Choose a strategy and solve.

3. Rhonda, Lian, Dwight, and Tom are members of a chess club. Each plays 2 times with each of the others. What is the total number of games they play?

_____

4. Bayard has 1 quarter, 5 dimes, and 8 nickels. He buys $0.75 worth of stamps and pays for them with 9 coins. What coins does he use?

_____

Mateo, Scott, and Caryn belong to their school's service club. Each has signed up for 10 hours of volunteer work. The table shows how many hours of service each student has given.

Name	Hours of Volunteer Work		
Mateo	$2\frac{1}{2}$	$3\frac{1}{5}$	
Scott	$1\frac{3}{4}$	$1\frac{1}{2}$	$2\frac{1}{4}$
Caryn	$1\frac{3}{4}$	$2\frac{1}{2}$	

5. Who has given more hours of service, Mateo or Scott? How many more?

_____

6. How many more hours must Caryn give to reach her goal of

10 hours? _____

WRITER'S CORNER

7. Make up a problem in which you use the numbers $1\frac{1}{2}$, $\frac{2}{3}$, and $\frac{1}{6}$. Then solve the problem.

_____

_____

Estimating Products

Estimate the product.

1. $\frac{4}{5}$ of 70 _____

2. $\frac{3}{5}$ of 88 _____

3. $\frac{3}{8}$ of 21 _____

4. $\frac{4}{7}$ of 420 _____

5. $\frac{19}{20}$ of 355 _____

6. $6\frac{1}{2} \times 2\frac{1}{4}$ _____

7. $2\frac{1}{3} \times 15\frac{2}{3}$ _____

8. $17\frac{1}{9} \times 3\frac{1}{3}$ _____

9. $65\frac{1}{6} \times 1\frac{8}{9}$ _____

Mixed Applications

10. Tyrone has filled $5\frac{7}{8}$ pages of his stamp book. Each page has room for 40 stamps. Estimate about how many stamps are in his book.

_____

11. It takes Alicia about $2\frac{1}{3}$ hours to assemble a model airplane. Can she assemble a model for each of 3 friends in 6 hours?

_____

VISUAL THINKING

Sandra drew this picture to model the product, $\frac{2}{3}$ of 13.

12. Sandra used 12 counters because 12 is compatible with 3, and 12 is close to what number?

_____

13. In Sandra's model each group represents what part of 12?

_____

14. Use Sandra's model to estimate $\frac{2}{3}$ of 13.

_____

Use the model to estimate the product. First circle the correct number of counters.

15. $\frac{5}{6}$ of 11 is about _____ .

16. $\frac{4}{5}$ of 17 is about _____ .

17. $\frac{5}{9}$ of 35 is about _____ .

29

Multiplying Fractions

Find the product. Write the answer in simplest form.

1. $\frac{1}{3} \times \frac{3}{8}$ _____

2. $\frac{2}{3} \times \frac{3}{5}$ _____

3. $\frac{5}{12} \times \frac{6}{7}$ _____

4. $\frac{2}{7} \times \frac{7}{8}$ _____

5. $\frac{5}{8} \times \frac{7}{10}$ _____

6. $\frac{4}{5} \times \frac{2}{7}$ _____

7. $\frac{1}{3} \times \frac{3}{5} \times \frac{5}{7}$ _____

8. $\frac{5}{2} \times \frac{2}{3} \times \frac{3}{10}$ _____

9. $\frac{3}{4} \times \frac{4}{5} \times \frac{1}{3}$ _____

10. $\frac{2}{3} \times \frac{7}{10} \times \frac{5}{21}$ _____

11. $\frac{9}{7} \times \frac{5}{9} \times \frac{21}{20}$ _____

12. $\frac{17}{6} \times \frac{5}{34} \times \frac{7}{10}$ _____

Complete. Write $<$, $>$, or $=$.

13. $\frac{6}{5} \times \frac{3}{5} \bigcirc \frac{3}{5}$

14. $\frac{3}{4} \times \frac{7}{8} \bigcirc \frac{7}{8}$

15. $\frac{4}{3} \times \frac{3}{8} \bigcirc \frac{1}{2}$

16. $\frac{3}{5} \times \frac{1}{6} \bigcirc \frac{1}{10}$

17. $\frac{1}{3} \times \frac{4}{5} \bigcirc \frac{4}{5}$

18. $\frac{3}{4} \times \frac{8}{9} \bigcirc \frac{2}{3}$

Mixed Applications

19. A gardener uses $\frac{2}{3}$ of a greenhouse for growing roses, with $\frac{3}{8}$ of this space for tea roses. What part of the space is used to grow tea roses?

_____

20. Tiffany spent $\frac{3}{5}$ of her money to buy begonias and $\frac{1}{2}$ of the remaining money to buy peas. What part of her money did she spend on peas?

_____

21. Marvella's uncle paid $26 for 20 plants. Some were carnations, selling at 4 for $3. The rest were zinnias priced at 3 for $5. How many plants of each type did he buy?

_____

NUMBER SENSE

Find the two numbers in each pair.

22. The sum of two numbers is 10. Their product is 1 less than 5^2.

_____

23. Two numbers differ by 4. Their product is 4 less than 7^2.

_____

30

Multiplying Mixed Numbers

Find the product.

1. $\frac{3}{4} \times 24$ _____

2. $7 \times 2\frac{1}{7}$ _____

3. $17 \times \frac{1}{3}$ _____

4. $9 \times 4\frac{1}{3}$ _____

5. $\frac{1}{2} \times 2\frac{1}{4}$ _____

6. $7\frac{1}{2} \times 1\frac{1}{3}$ _____

7. $6\frac{2}{3} \times 2\frac{1}{4}$ _____

8. $2\frac{2}{3} \times 3\frac{1}{8}$ _____

9. $\frac{3}{7} \times 5\frac{1}{4}$ _____

10. $2 \times 6\frac{2}{5}$ _____

11. $4\frac{1}{3} \times 1\frac{1}{2}$ _____

12. $2\frac{4}{7} \times \frac{5}{9}$ _____

13. $3\frac{1}{5} \times 2\frac{1}{4}$ _____

14. $9\frac{3}{4} \times 2\frac{2}{13}$ _____

15. $37\frac{1}{2} \times 1\frac{3}{5}$ _____

16. $\frac{5}{8} \times 1\frac{4}{5} \times 1\frac{7}{9}$ _____

17. $1\frac{1}{3} \times 1\frac{2}{5} \times 1\frac{1}{2}$ _____

18. $\frac{1}{3} \times \frac{1}{7} \times 4\frac{2}{3}$ _____

19. $5 \times 2\frac{1}{10} \times 2\frac{1}{7}$ _____

Mixed Applications

20. At the circus $\frac{1}{8}$ of the performers were trapeze artists. Of these, $\frac{2}{3}$ were women. What part of the circus performers were women trapeze artists?

_____

21. Jim and his uncle went to the circus. Together they spent $30, $\frac{4}{15}$ of that for a bus ride, $\frac{2}{5}$ for food, $7 for tickets, and the rest on souvenirs. What part of their money did they spend on souvenirs?

_____

NUMBER SENSE

Fill in two numbers that make the inequality true.

22. Use multiples of 3 that differ by 3. $(\frac{2}{3} \times$ _____$) < 11 < (\frac{2}{3} \times$ _____$)$

23. Use multiples of 4 that differ by 4. $(\frac{3}{4} \times$ _____$) < 17 < (\frac{3}{4} \times$ _____$)$

24. Use multiples of 5 that differ by 5. $(\frac{4}{5} \times$ _____$) < 30 < (\frac{4}{5} \times$ _____$)$

31

Estimating Quotients

Choose the best estimate. Write **a**, **b**, or **c**.

1. $12 \div 2\frac{4}{5}$ **a.** 2   **b.** 3   **c.** 4   _____

2. $15\frac{1}{8} \div 2\frac{5}{6}$ **a.** 5   **b.** 7   **c.** 8   _____

3. $100 \div 23\frac{1}{2}$ **a.** 3   **b.** 4   **c.** 5   _____

4. $47\frac{7}{8} \div 3\frac{1}{7}$ **a.** 12   **b.** 14   **c.** 16   _____

Estimate the quotient.

5. $20 \div 4\frac{4}{5}$ _____

6. $45 \div 2\frac{8}{9}$ _____

7. $72 \div 8\frac{1}{6}$ _____

8. $55\frac{1}{5} \div 4\frac{9}{10}$ _____

9. $35\frac{4}{5} \div 9\frac{1}{8}$ _____

10. $48\frac{2}{5} \div 5\frac{4}{5}$ _____

11. $31\frac{5}{6} \div 16\frac{1}{6}$ _____

12. $59\frac{4}{7} \div 2\frac{1}{7}$ _____

13. $74\frac{7}{10} \div 3\frac{1}{10}$ _____

Mixed Applications

14. During a storm $8\frac{1}{2}$ inches of snow fell in $3\frac{1}{4}$ hours. About how many inches of snow fell in 1 hour?

_____

15. The fees at a skating rink were $2.75 for children, $3.50 for adults, and $1.50 for renting skates. A group of 5 people paid $14.50 to skate. All brought their own skates. How many were children?

_____

NUMBER SENSE

16. Check that $\frac{3+3}{3} + \frac{3}{3 \times 3} + \frac{3+3}{3 \times 3} = 3$. _____

Then use ten twos to write an expression equal to 2.

_____

Exploring Division with Fractions

Use the fraction-bar model for each division. Write the quotient.

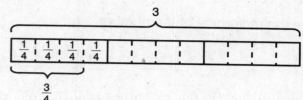

1. $3 \div \frac{3}{4}$ _____

2. $2 \div \frac{1}{4}$ _____

3. $2\frac{1}{4} \div \frac{1}{4}$ _____

Use the number line to model each division. Write the quotient.

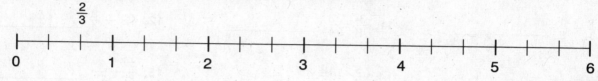

4. $2 \div \frac{2}{3}$ _____

5. $6 \div \frac{2}{3}$ _____

6. $5\frac{1}{3} \div \frac{4}{3}$ _____

Use equivalent fractions and the fraction-bar model to find the quotient.

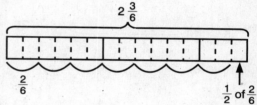

7. Count how many groups of $\frac{2}{6}$ are in $2\frac{3}{6}$.

   $2\frac{1}{2} \div \frac{1}{3}$ _____

8. Count how many groups of $\frac{3}{12}$ are in $\frac{10}{12}$.

   $\frac{5}{6} \div \frac{1}{4}$ _____

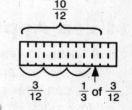

Think of a number line to model each division. Write the quotient.

9. $4 \div \frac{2}{3}$ _____

10. $2\frac{2}{3} \div \frac{1}{3}$ _____

11. $3\frac{1}{3} \div \frac{2}{3}$ _____

Think of fraction bars to model each division. Use equivalent fractions if necessary. Write the quotient.

12. $3 \div \frac{1}{2}$ _____

13. $5 \div \frac{1}{4}$ _____

14. $\frac{1}{2} \div \frac{1}{6}$ _____

VISUAL THINKING

15. Look for a pattern. Draw the missing rectangle.

Dividing Fractions

Write the reciprocal of the number.

1. $\frac{1}{7}$ _____   2. 6 _____   3. $1\frac{1}{8}$ _____   4. $3\frac{1}{3}$ _____   5. $2\frac{1}{4}$ _____   6. $\frac{2}{5}$ _____

Find the quotient. Write the answer in simplest form.

7. $6 \div \frac{1}{2}$ _____   8. $7 \div \frac{1}{3}$ _____   9. $\frac{3}{5} \div \frac{1}{4}$ _____

10. $\frac{1}{3} \div \frac{1}{9}$ _____   11. $\frac{3}{8} \div \frac{3}{4}$ _____   12. $12 \div \frac{3}{4}$ _____

13. $\frac{1}{4} \div \frac{1}{5}$ _____   14. $\frac{5}{12} \div \frac{2}{3}$ _____   15. $\frac{7}{8} \div \frac{1}{2}$ _____

16. $\frac{8}{9} \div \frac{1}{3}$ _____   17. $\frac{7}{8} \div \frac{1}{8}$ _____   18. $\frac{3}{10} \div \frac{2}{5}$ _____

19. $\frac{1}{5} \div \frac{7}{10}$ _____   20. $\frac{9}{2} \div \frac{3}{4}$ _____   21. $\frac{3}{5} \div \frac{6}{1}$ _____

Complete.

22. $0.2 \times$ _____ $= 1$ 23. $0.1 \times$ _____ $= 1$ 24. $0.125 \times$ _____ $= 1$

Mixed Applications

25. A library in Washington, D.C., has a Dial-a-Story program. When you call, you can hear a $3\frac{1}{2}$-minute folktale. How many times can the complete story be repeated in 1 hour?

_____

26. A library shelf is 9 feet wide. A set of nature books fills $\frac{1}{6}$ of the shelf space. Each book in the set is $\frac{3}{5}$-inch thick. How many books are in the set?

_____

MIXED REVIEW

Write in scientific notation.

1. 6,420 _____   2. 65,000,000 _____

Write in standard form.

3. 2.0×10^6 _____   4. 4.15×10^2 _____

34

Dividing Mixed Numbers

Find the quotient. Write the answer in simplest form.

1. $\frac{1}{3} \div 5$ _____

2. $1\frac{3}{5} \div \frac{3}{5}$ _____

3. $2\frac{1}{8} \div \frac{1}{4}$ _____

4. $\frac{2}{3} \div 2\frac{1}{3}$ _____

5. $\frac{5}{6} \div 1\frac{1}{4}$ _____

6. $8 \div 5\frac{1}{3}$ _____

7. $3\frac{4}{7} \div \frac{5}{7}$ _____

8. $21 \div 2\frac{1}{3}$ _____

9. $5\frac{1}{4} \div \frac{1}{2}$ _____

10. $\frac{7}{8} \div 1\frac{1}{6}$ _____

11. $1\frac{3}{5} \div 8$ _____

12. $15 \div 2\frac{1}{12}$ _____

13. $9\frac{3}{4} \div 1\frac{5}{8}$ _____

14. $7\frac{5}{6} \div \frac{5}{6}$ _____

15. $5\frac{1}{2} \div \frac{1}{6}$ _____

16. $10\frac{2}{5} \div 2\frac{3}{5}$ _____

17. $7\frac{1}{3} \div \frac{5}{6}$ _____

18. $15\frac{3}{4} \div 3\frac{1}{2}$ _____

19. $16\frac{2}{3} \div 6\frac{1}{4}$ _____

20. $12\frac{3}{5} \div \frac{9}{10}$ _____

21. $1\frac{3}{4} \div 4\frac{2}{3}$ _____

22. $9\frac{3}{4} \div 2\frac{1}{6}$ _____

23. $\frac{3}{10} \div 2\frac{2}{5}$ _____

24. $4\frac{4}{5} \div 1\frac{4}{5}$ _____

25. $3\frac{1}{21} \div 2\frac{2}{7}$ _____

26. $11\frac{1}{9} \div \frac{5}{6}$ _____

27. $8\frac{1}{6} \div 2\frac{1}{3}$ _____

Mixed Applications

28. Lee has a $1\frac{1}{2}$-pound supply of Kitty Biscuit Treats. Each day he gives his kitten $\frac{1}{8}$ pound of the biscuits. For how many days will his supply last?

_____

29. Lee's kitten, Sophia, is $2\frac{1}{3}$ times as heavy as she was last year. Sophia now weighs 21 ounces. What did she weigh a year ago?

_____

LOGICAL REASONING

30. Find the numbers $\triangle$ and $\square$ if $(1\frac{3}{5} \times \triangle) + (\frac{3}{5} \times \square) = 5$
and $(1\frac{3}{5} \times \square) + (\frac{3}{5} \times \triangle) = 6$.

$\triangle =$ _____ $\square =$ _____

Problem Solving
Multistep Problems

1. Inés paid $36 for swimming lessons. Each lesson lasted $\frac{3}{4}$ hour and cost $4. How many hours of swimming lessons did Wendy have?

2. Last month Hilary played 15 games of tennis. She won 3 more games than she lost. Keith won $1\frac{1}{3}$ times the number of games that Hilary won. How many games did Keith win?

_____

| Mixed Applications | STRATEGIES | • Solve a Simpler Problem • Draw a Picture • Find a Pattern • Guess and Check |

Choose a strategy and solve.

3. Dennis rode his bicycle around a circular path $4\frac{1}{2}$ miles long. He started at the gate house and rode 7 miles in the same direction before he stopped for a rest. How far did he have to go to reach the gate house again?

4. A farmer has 600 feet of wire to make a fence for one side of his garden. The fence will have 3 strands of wire attached to posts 8 feet apart. How many fence posts will be needed?

_____

LOGICAL REASONING

5. The numbers in each square have separate patterns across and down. Look for the patterns and fill in the missing numbers.

6. Describe any patterns you see along the diagonals of the squares for Exercise 5.

_____

$\frac{5}{4}$		5	10
		1	2
		$\frac{1}{5}$	$\frac{2}{5}$
$\frac{1}{100}$			$\frac{2}{25}$

Introduction to Algebra

Write $<$, $>$, $\leq$, $\geq$, $\neq$, or $=$.

1. $25 + 3^2$ $\bigcirc$ 34

2. $12.6 - 5.7$ $\bigcirc$ 4.1

3. 15×6 $\bigcirc$ 96

4. $132 \div 11$ $\bigcirc$ 11

5. $91 - 4^2$ $\bigcirc$ 25

6. $16 + 28$ $\bigcirc$ $4(11)$

7. $121 \div 11$ $\bigcirc$ 13

8. 1.2×1.5 $\bigcirc$ 1.8

9. $8^2 + 2^2$ $\bigcirc$ 10^2

10. $5^2 - 4^2$ $\bigcirc$ 3^2

11. 0.041 $\bigcirc$ 0.41

12. 56 $\bigcirc$ 55 $\bigcirc$ 54

Use any of the numbers 3, 5, and 6 to write a numerical expression for the given value.

13. 27

_____

14. 13

_____

15. 48

_____

Write an example of each.

16. algebraic expression

_____

17. algebraic equation

_____

18. algebraic inequality

_____

Mixed Applications

19. Write a numerical expression using division that shows what fraction of one dollar a penny is.

_____

20. Stan buys $5\frac{2}{3}$ yards of material at $12 per yard. What is the total cost of the material?

_____

MIXED REVIEW

Compute.

1. $15.653 - 3.92$

_____

2. 65.01×2.1

_____

3. $1.323 \div 2.45$

_____

Order of Operations

Use mental math and the order of operations to find the value of the expression.

1. $21 + 29 - 25$ _____

2. $36 \div 9 - 2$ _____

3. $48 \div (6 \times 2)$ _____

4. $4 \times 3 + 2 - 7$ _____

5. $45 \div 15 + 2 \times 3$ _____

6. $2 \times (18.9 - 7.4)$ _____

Find the value of the expression. You may want to use a calculator.

7. $18^2 - 30 \div 15 \times 9$

_____

8. $12.8 + 6 \times 3^2 - 4^3$

_____

9. $(54 - 3) \div 17 + 63 \div 9$

_____

Insert parentheses where necessary to make each equation true.

10. $3 \times 8 - 5 = 9$

_____

11. $20 + 12 \div 4 + 4 = 4$

_____

12. $15 - 3 \div 12 + 1 = 2$

_____

Mixed Applications

Write a number sentence. Solve.

13. The members of the swimming team have heights of 182 cm, 157 cm, 165 cm, 146 cm, and 178 cm. Find the mean and the median of their heights.

_____

_____

14. When the 13-member basketball team stopped at a restaurant for lunch, they ordered 5 cheeseburgers at $1.29 each, 5 sandwiches at $1.89 each, 3 salads at $2.79 apiece, and 13 drinks at $0.89 apiece. How much did the team pay for lunch in all?

_____

_____

NUMBER SENSE

15. Write the next number in the following pattern.
1, 2, 4, 7, 11, 16, 22

_____

Expressions
Addition and Subtraction

Evaluate the expression for $x = 5$.

1. $x + 2.7$ _____

2. $x + 12$ _____

3. $x - 3\frac{4}{7}$ _____

Evaluate the expression for $n = 15$.

4. $n - 6$ _____

5. $52 - n$ _____

6. $n - 15 + 15$ _____

Write the algebraic expression.

7. 19 less than a number, t

_____

8. thirty-four increased by the sum of thirteen and a number, n

_____

Write each expression in words.

9. $t - 7$

_____

10. $29 + n$

_____

11. $23 - r$

_____

12. $c + (5 + 22)$

_____

Mixed Applications

13. Danielle has n dollars in her wallet. She pays $5.19 for a book. What expression shows how much money she has left?

_____

14. Find all the numbers that are less than 200 and have the prime factors 3, 5, and 13.

_____

VISUAL THINKING

15. The number line is marked in whole numbers. Use the variable d to write expressions for points A and B.

_____

Mental Math and Number Properties

Name the property illustrated.

1. $3 \cdot x = x \cdot 3$

_____

2. $3 \cdot (x + 3) = (3 \cdot x) + (3 \cdot 3)$

_____

3. $k + 0 = k$

_____

4. $12 + (3 + r) = (12 + 3) + r$

_____

Find the value of n.

5. $6 + (3 + n) = (6 + 3) + 8$ _____

6. $7 \cdot (3 + n) = 7 \cdot 3 + 7 \cdot 4$ _____

Use mental math to find the value.

7. $(21\frac{1}{7})(7)$ _____

8. $21\frac{5}{8}(7\frac{5}{9} - 7\frac{5}{9})$ _____

Write *true* or *false*. Justify your answer.

9. $\frac{1}{5} \cdot z = 5 \cdot z$

_____

10. $3 \cdot (x - 1) = 3x - 3$

_____

Mixed Applications

11. Ryan started practice with 15 tennis balls. At the end of practice he could only find 9 of the balls. Write in simplest form the fraction of his tennis balls that Ryan lost.

_____

12. Juanita gave one of her friends three tapes and another friend r tapes. She paid $7 for each tape. Write two expressions for the amount of money she paid for the tapes she gave her friends.

_____

LOGICAL REASONING

13. This sequence of numbers has a pattern. Find the pattern.   1   2   3   5   8   13   21   34   55

_____

Exploring Equations

There are 9 cubes in the right pan and 2 cubes visible in the left pan. Let c = the number of cubes under the handkerchief in the left pan. The pans are balanced.

1. Write an algebraic expression to describe how many cubes you have on the left pan.

    _____

2. Write an equation to describe the relationship between the number of cubes in the left pan and the number of cubes in the right pan.

    _____

3. Suppose you remove 2 cubes from each pan. How many cubes are now on the right pan?

    _____

4. How many cubes must now be on the left pan?

    _____

5. What is the value of the variable c?

    _____

6. Explain how you would find the number of cubes under the handkerchief on the pan balance.

    _____

Solve each equation.

7. $x + 9 = 21$ _____

8. $c + 7 = 14$ _____

9. $3 + a = 6$ _____

WRITER'S CORNER

10. Write a word sentence to describe Problem 6.

    _____

    _____

Addition Equations

Solve the equation. Check your solution.

1. $n + 8 = 13$

_____

2. $b + 17 = 62$

_____

3. $x + \frac{5}{6} = 7\frac{1}{6}$

_____

4. $y + \frac{1}{7} = \frac{5}{8}$

_____

5. $14 + y = 69$

_____

6. $c + 3.6 = 4.9$

_____

Write and solve an equation. Use the variable n.

7. A number increased by 19 is 221.

_____

8. A number increased by $1\frac{2}{3}$ is 8.

_____

9. The sum of a number and $6\frac{1}{5}$ is $8\frac{2}{3}$.

_____

10. 5.4 more than a number is 23.1.

_____

11. A number increased by the sum of 3 and 2.6 is 9.

_____

12. 29 more than a number is 113.

_____

Mixed Applications

13. Lita jogged $2\frac{2}{3}$ miles more on Wednesday than on Tuesday. She jogged $4\frac{1}{2}$ miles on Wednesday. Write and solve an equation to find how many miles she jogged on Tuesday.

_____

14. A wildlife refuge has about 10^5 elk. Are there more than or fewer than 1 million elk in the refuge?

_____

MIXED REVIEW

Find the product or quotient.

1. $9\frac{3}{5} \div 3\frac{1}{5}$ _____

2. $4.8 \div 12$ _____

3. $32\frac{1}{2} \times 2\frac{2}{13}$ _____

Subtraction Equations

Solve the equation. Check your solution.

1. $a - 65 = 7$

_____

2. $x - 58 = 16$

_____

3. $x - 4\frac{3}{8} = 6$

_____

4. $c - 42 = 67$

_____

5. $y - 4.8 = 9.2$

_____

6. $b - 4\frac{1}{4} = 2\frac{2}{3}$

_____

Use addition or subtraction to solve the equation.
Check your solution.

7. $a - 2\frac{2}{9} = 1\frac{1}{2}$

_____

8. $c - 6.005 = 2.5$

_____

9. $b + 55 = 83$

_____

Mixed Applications

Write an equation for each problem. Use the variable m.
Then solve.

10. Five students are absent from math class today. If there are 22 students in math class today, how many students would there be if none were absent?

_____

11. Juan pays $22.05 more than Kim each month for his health club membership. Juan pays $58.95 each month. How much does Kim pay each month?

_____

_____

VISUAL THINKING

12. Carl had part of a pizza. He gave $\frac{1}{6}$ of a pizza to Susan. He still had the amount shown. What part of a pizza did Carl have at first? Use the variable p.

_____

Solve the equation for p.

_____

43

Expressions
Multiplication and Division

Evaluate the expression $\frac{z}{8}$ for the values shown.

1. $z = 19.2$

2. $z = 92$

3. $z = 16.016$

4. $z = 5\frac{4}{9}$

_____

Evaluate each expression. Let $m = 32$ and $n = 150$.

5. $\frac{m}{16}$ _____

6. $2n - 200$ _____

7. $\frac{3}{4}m - 12$ _____

Write an algebraic expression for each word expression.

8. the product of 14 and a number, x

_____

9. a number, n, divided by 9

_____

Write each expression in words.

10. $\frac{z}{11}$

_____

11. $z + 11$

_____

Mixed Applications

12. The amount of cashews in a mixture of nuts is 3 times the amount of almonds. Let c represent the amount of cashews in the mixture. If there are $1\frac{1}{2}$ lb of almonds in the nut mixture, how many pounds of cashews are there?

_____

13. Josh is one-third as old as his mother. If Josh's mother is 45 years old, how old is Josh?

_____

SCIENCE CONNECTION

14. The formula for distance is $d = r \cdot t$, where $d =$ distance, $r =$ rate, and $t =$ time. If a car travels for 15 seconds at 88 feet per second, how far will it have traveled?

_____

Multiplication Equations

Solve the equation. Check your solution.

1. $6n = 42$

2. $3y = 192$

3. $8x = 72$

4. $4y = 28$

5. $7n = 112$

6. $8x = 272$

7. $7n = 49$

8. $33y = 66$

9. $6b = 96$

10. $5n = 280$

11. $6n = 72$

12. $13r = 169$

13. $5.4k = 21.6$

14. $4.5a = 9.0$

15. $4.8b = 36$

Mixed Applications

Write an equation for each problem using the variable n. Then solve and check the equation.

16. Akio has 84 baseball cards. This is 19 fewer cards than Mike has. How many baseball cards does Mike have?

17. Janelle can ride her bike 3 times as fast as Michelle can jog. If Janelle rides her bike at a rate of 12 miles per hour, how fast can Michelle jog?

NUMBER SENSE • MENTAL MATH

Study each equation. Then solve it mentally.

18. $5 + r = 6 - r$

19. $z - 16 = -16$

20. $7n - 7 = 0$

Problem-Solving Strategy
Use a Formula

Use a formula to solve.

1. A motorboat travels across a river at a rate of 15 meters per second. If the river is 1,350 meters wide, how long will it take the boat to cross the river?

   _____

2. The Barbly family want to go a distance of 440 miles in one day. They drive at an average rate of 55 miles per hour. How long will the journey take?

   _____

3. A swimmer can swim at a rate of 8 meters per second. How far can he swim in $1\frac{1}{2}$ minutes?

   _____

4. The rate of a jet airliner is 650 miles per hour. Find the distance traveled in 2 hours.

   _____

Mixed Applications ➤ **STRATEGIES** • Use a Formula • Draw a Diagram • Write a Number Sentence • Guess and Check

Choose a strategy and solve.

5. Aretha has a total of 15 quarters and dimes. The total value of the coins is $1.95. How many of each coin does she have?

   _____

6. A small plane travels at a rate of 125 kilometers per hour. Find the distance traveled in 3 hours.

   _____

7. Bo took a walk. From his home, he went 2 blocks west, 7 blocks north, 3 blocks west, 4 blocks south, and 5 blocks east. How far was he from his home?

   _____

8. Domingo has saved $296.55 to buy a go-cart. The go-cart costs $450.00. How much money does he still need?

   _____

WRITER'S CORNER

9. Write a word problem that can be solved with the equation $2x = 10$.

   _____

   _____

Division Equations

Solve the equation. Check your solution.

1. $\frac{x}{4} = 9$

_____

2. $\frac{a}{5} = 7$

_____

3. $\frac{n}{3} = 29$

_____

4. $\frac{n}{3} = 10$

_____

5. $\frac{x}{5} = 24$

_____

6. $\frac{b}{9} = 15$

_____

7. $\frac{n}{7} = 17$

_____

8. $\frac{x}{3} = 8$

_____

9. $\frac{y}{5} = 33$

_____

10. $\frac{e}{36} = 5$

_____

11. $\frac{a}{25} = 4$

_____

12. $\frac{b}{16} = 7$

_____

Mixed Applications

Write an equation for Exercises 13–16, using the variable *n*.
Then solve and check the solution.

13. If a number, *n,* divided by 8 equals 2.5, what is *n*?

_____

14. The sum of a number, *n,* and 6.05 is 12.4. What is *n*?

_____

15. Stacy is one-fourth as old as her mother. If Stacy's mother is 36, how old is Stacy?

_____

16. One-third of a painting job takes 24 hours. How long will it take to complete the entire job?

_____

NUMBER SENSE • ESTIMATION

Use compatible numbers to estimate the solution.

17. $6b = 110$

_____

18. $4n = 159$

_____

19. $\frac{14}{x} = 5$

_____

Exploring Inequalities

1. Write an inequality to describe the relationship between the number of cubes on the left pan and the number of cubes on the right pan. (Let $c =$ the number of cubes under the handkerchief.)

_____

2. Explain how you would find the possible numbers of cubes under the handkerchief.

_____

3. Solve the inequality.

_____

4. Explain how to find the possible numbers of cubes under the handkerchief on the pan balance.

_____

Solve each inequality.

5. $y + 7 < 11$

_____

6. $n + 2 > 4$

_____

7. $z + 3 < 8$

_____

MIXED REVIEW

Use equivalent fractions to compare. Write $<$, $>$, or $=$.

1. $\frac{2}{3}$ ◯ $\frac{6}{7}$

2. $\frac{3}{5}$ ◯ $\frac{4}{7}$

3. $\frac{6}{5}$ ◯ $\frac{5}{4}$

Find the product.

4. $\begin{array}{r} 56 \\ \times 0.2 \\ \hline \end{array}$

5. $\begin{array}{r} 0.5 \\ \times 0.5 \\ \hline \end{array}$

6. $\begin{array}{r} 1.4 \\ \times\ \ 3 \\ \hline \end{array}$

7. $\begin{array}{r} 0.002 \\ \times\ \ \ 4.1 \\ \hline \end{array}$

8. $\begin{array}{r} 0.73 \\ \times\ 4.6 \\ \hline \end{array}$

Geometry
Around You

When you look at a photograph of the U.S. Supreme Court, you can imagine many geometric figures. Some are pictured below. Refer to these drawings and use geometric words to complete Exercises 1–3.

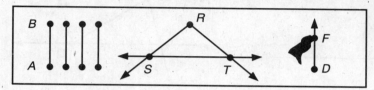

1. The columns suggest

    _____ _____

    like $\overline{AB}$.

2. On the pediment above

    the columns, you can

    imagine an _____ like

    $\angle$ SRT and a

    _____ like $\overleftrightarrow{ST}$.

3. You can think of a

    flagpole as continuing

    upward, suggesting a

    _____ like $\overrightarrow{DF}$.

Use letters to name the geometric figure.

4.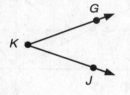

    _____

5.

    _____

6.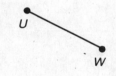

    _____

Complete each statement.

7. The surface of a desk is part of a

    _____ .

8. When you open a pair of scissors, the

    blades form an _____ .

VISUAL THINKING

9. Look across and down for words
   that name geometric ideas.
   Draw loops around six words.
   Some loops will overlap.

```
S  A  A  R  A  M  P  S
O  P  L  A  N  E  O  U
A  P  O  Y  G  V  I  P
R  L  N  E  L  I  N  E
S  E  G  M  E  N  T  R
```

Applications
Geometric Relationships

Use the drawings for Exercises 1–9.

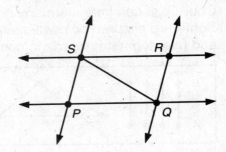

1. Name two rays with endpoint R. _____

2. Name three line segments that
   have S as one endpoint. _____

3. Name two pairs of lines that
   appear parallel. _____

Identify each pair of lines as *skew, parallel,*
or *intersecting.*

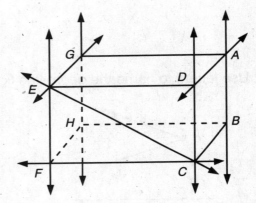

4. $\overleftrightarrow{AB}$, $\overleftrightarrow{DC}$

   _____

5. $\overleftrightarrow{DA}$, $\overleftrightarrow{EC}$

   _____

6. $\overleftrightarrow{DA}$, $\overleftrightarrow{AB}$

   _____

7. $\overleftrightarrow{EF}$, $\overleftrightarrow{DC}$

   _____

8. $\overleftrightarrow{ED}$, $\overleftrightarrow{GA}$

   _____

9. $\overleftrightarrow{EG}$, $\overleftrightarrow{FC}$

   _____

Mixed Applications

10. Draw three lines that intersect at
    point P.

    P •

11. Draw three lines so that points R, S,
    and T are intersection points.

    • R

    • S

    • T

NUMBER SENSE

12. Sara weighs $\frac{3}{4}$ of her brother's weight, minus 12 pounds.
    What is her brother's weight? What is Sara's weight?

    _____

Lines and Line Segments

Use the dots at the right for Exercises 1 and 2.

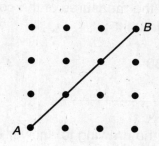

1. Draw two <u>congruent</u> line segments that <u>are</u> both parallel to $\overline{AB}$ and two-thirds as long as $\overline{AB}$.

2. Draw a line segment <u>that</u> is both congruent to $\overline{AB}$ and perpendicular to $\overline{AB}$.

Identify the two line segments as *parallel, perpendicular,* or *neither.* Also, tell whether the line segments are *congruent.*

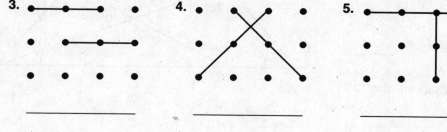

3. _____

_____

4. _____

_____

5. _____

_____

6. _____

_____

7. Bisect $\overline{HQ}$.

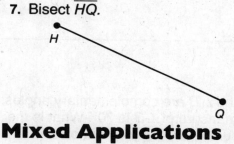

8. Construct a line perpendicular to $\overleftrightarrow{CD}$ at point *E.*

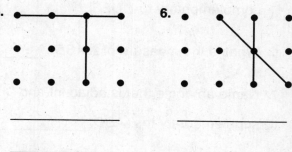

Mixed Applications

Complete the statements in Exercises 9 and 10.

9. If $\overline{RS}$ bisects $\overline{XY}$ at *P,* then

$\overline{XP} \cong$ _____ .

10. If $\overleftrightarrow{AB}$ is perpendicular to $\overleftrightarrow{CD}$ and $\overleftrightarrow{CD}$ is perpendicular to $\overleftrightarrow{EF}$, then $\overleftrightarrow{AB}$ is

_____ to $\overleftrightarrow{EF}$.

LOGICAL REASONING

11. How many bisectors would you need to construct if you start with a 12-inch line segment and want to construct a $\frac{3}{8}$-inch line segment?

_____

Angles and Their Measures

Give the measures of the complement and the supplement of each angle.

1. 80°

2. 25°

3. 68°

4. 43°

_____ _____ _____ _____

Use the drawing to answer Exercises 5–9.

5. Name an angle that is adjacent and
   complementary to ∠DEF. _____

6. What is the measure of ∠ABD? _____

7. Name an angle that is adjacent and
   supplementary to ∠ABD. _____

8. Name an angle that is supplementary
   to ∠EFD but not adjacent to ∠EFD.

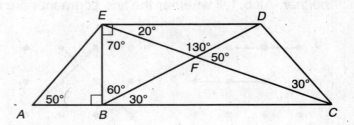

9. Name two pairs of vertical angles.

_____

Mixed Applications

10. At 4:00, what are the measures of the
    two angles formed by the hands of a
    clock?

    _____

11. ∠A and ∠B are complementary angles.
    The measure of ∠B is 70°. What is the
    measure of the supplement of ∠A?

    _____

12. The measure of ∠APB is 20°. When $\overrightarrow{PC}$ is drawn, ∠BPC
    measures 50°. What is the measure of ∠APC? There are two
    possible answers. Show two ways to draw $\overrightarrow{PC}$ and give both
    answers.

measure of

∠APC: _____

measure of

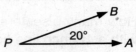

∠APC: _____

Measuring and Constructing Angles

Use a protractor to measure each angle.

1.

2.

3.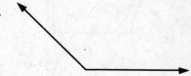

Use a protractor to draw each angle.

4. m∠ABC = 70°

5. m∠DEF = 30°

6. m∠GHI = 105°

Use a compass and straightedge to construct a congruent angle.

7.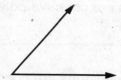

8.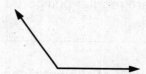

Mixed Applications

9. ∠A and ∠B are supplementary. ∠A is congruent to ∠C. If ∠C measures 115°, what is the measure of ∠B?

_____

10. When Lynn exercises her dog, she starts walking north. Then she makes three right turns and heads home. In what direction is she going?

_____

VISUAL THINKING

11. How many angles are in the figure? (Count ∠APG only once.)

_____

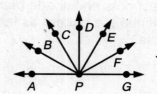

Polygons

Identify each figure as a *concave polygon*, a *convex polygon*, or *neither*.

1.

   _____

   _____

2.

   _____

   _____

3.

   _____

   _____

Connect dots to complete each polygon.

4. polygon with 4 congruent sides

   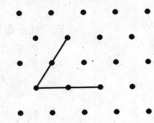

5. regular polygon with 6 sides

   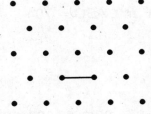

Write *true* or *false*.

6. All squares are regular polygons.

   _____

7. Some triangles are concave polygons.

   _____

8. All polygons with congruent sides are regular polygons.

   _____

9. Some 4-sided polygons are concave.

   _____

10. A 5-sided polygon has exactly 5 diagonals.

    _____

11. A 6-sided polygon has exactly 6 diagonals.

    _____

VISUAL THINKING

12. Connect dots and shade triangles to continue the pattern as far as possible.

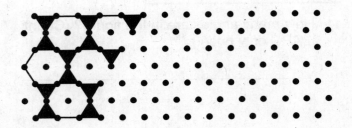

Problem-Solving Strategy
Find a Pattern

1. When Nora designs patterns shaped like regular polygons, she counts all line segments, diagonals, and sides. For a square, she counts 2 diagonals and 4 sides, or 6 line segments. What is the total number of line segments for a pentagon?

_____

2. In counting diagonals and sides for her designs with regular polygons, how many line segments does Nora find if her pattern is shaped like an equilateral

   triangle? _____

   a regular hexagon? _____

   a regular nonagon (9 sides)?

   _____

Mixed Applications

STRATEGIES	• Guess and Check • Work Backward
	• Make a Model • Draw a Diagram
	• Find a Pattern

Choose a strategy and solve.

3. Mark took a trip from Lyle to Clark. He went $\frac{1}{15}$ of the way by subway, $\frac{5}{6}$ of the way by train, and 2 miles by bus. How many miles long was his trip?

_____

4. At the railroad station, Mark bought a round-trip ticket for $16.50. This cost $2.50 less than the price of two single tickets. How much was a single ticket?

_____

5. Amy packs gift boxes of fruit. In one layer she puts rows of 2 grapefruit between rows of 3 oranges. There are twice as many oranges as grapefruit. What is the least number of oranges in one layer? the least number of grapefruit?

_____

6. When 25 students went to Washington, D.C., 18 of them visited the Museum of Natural History and 22 visited the National Air and Space Museum. How many students visited both museums?

_____

NUMBER SENSE

Look for a pattern in the triangular numbers.

triangular numbers   1   3   6   10

7. Find the 5th, 6th, and 10th triangular numbers. _____ , _____ , _____

Triangles

Classify each triangle according to the measures of its angles.

1. 55°, 25°, 100°

_____

2. 68°, 90°, 22°

_____

3. 20°, 75°, 85°

_____

4. 25°, 70°, 85°

_____

5. 50°, 40°, 90°

_____

6. 30°, 60°, 90°

_____

7. 110°, 30°, 40°

_____

8. 45°, 45°, 90°

_____

9. 42°, 78°, 60°

_____

10. 40°, 50°, 90°

_____

11. 91°, 44°, 45°

_____

12. 15°, 82°, 83°

_____

Classify each triangle according to the lengths of its sides.

13. 15 ft, 12 ft, 15 ft

_____

14. 7 m, 9 m, 11 m

_____

15. 8 cm, 5 cm, 8 cm

_____

16. 14 cm, 9 cm, 7 cm

_____

17. 10 m, 6 m, 10 m

_____

18. 12 ft, 12 ft, 12 ft

_____

Mixed Applications

19. In a triangle, the angle measures have a sum of 180°. If one angle measures 30° and the second angle has twice the measure of the third angle, what are the measures of the second and third angles?

_____

20. Tai is fencing a triangular garden plot. He wants 5 posts along each side. What is the least number of posts that Tai will need?

_____

VISUAL THINKING

21. Draw line segments to show how the figure can be separated into 8 congruent equilateral triangles.

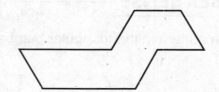

Constructing Triangles

Use the congruent triangles *QNP* and *RCK* to answer
Exercises 1–4.

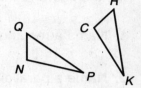

1. $\overline{NP}$ ≅ line segment _____

2. $\overline{QP}$ ≅ line segment _____

3. $\overline{QN}$ ≅ line segment _____

4. △*PNQ* ≅ △_____

Use the given segments to construct each triangle. Classify
each triangle by the lengths of the sides.

5.
___3 cm___

___3 cm___

___3 cm___

_____

6.
___2.5 cm___

___4.5 cm___

___4.5 cm___

_____

7.
___2.5 cm___

___3 cm___

___4 cm___

_____

Mixed Applications

8. In a right triangle, one of the acute
angles measures 40° more than the
other. What is the measure of each
acute angle?

_____

9. Complete: Two sides of a triangle
measure 5 cm and 9 cm. The third side
must be greater than 4 cm long and

less than _____ cm long.

VISUAL THINKING

10. Connect dots to draw a triangle congruent to the
given triangle. (HINT: There are three different ways
to draw the triangle.)

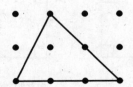

Exploring Relationships Among Quadrilaterals

Use the figure at the right for Exercises 1–3.

1. Name a rectangle. _____

2. Name a parallelogram that is not a

   rectangle. _____

3. Name three trapezoids.

   _____

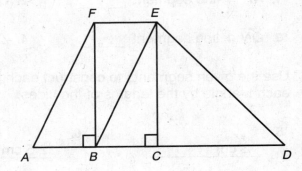

Identify each figure by writing *quadrilateral, trapezoid, parallelogram, rectangle, rhombus,* or *square.*

4. A parallelogram with congruent sides

   is a _____ .

5. A quadrilateral with just one pair of parallel sides is a

   _____ .

Write *always, sometimes,* or *never.*

6. A rhombus is a square.

   _____

7. A square is a rhombus.

   _____

8. A trapezoid is a parallelogram.

   _____

9. A polygon is a quadrilateral.

   _____

VISUAL THINKING

Draw one line segment in each figure to form the two figures described.

10.

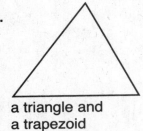

a triangle and
a trapezoid

11.

two trapezoids

12.

a trapezoid and
a rectangle

Problem Solving
Choose a Strategy

Mixed Applications

STRATEGIES

• Draw a Diagram • Guess and Check
• Work Backward • Find a Pattern
• Make a Table • Use a Formula

Choose a strategy and solve.

Use a formula to solve.

Michelle designs jewelry. The design at the right shows an equilateral triangle inside a regular hexagon.

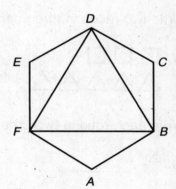

1. What is the measure of each angle of the hexagon?

   _____

2. What is the sum of the angle measures of the hexagon?

   _____

3. What is the measure of $\angle DFB$?

   _____

4. What is the measure of $\angle ABF$?

   _____

Another design shows an isosceles triangle inside a regular pentagon.

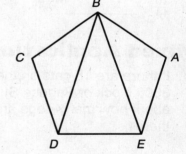

5. What is the measure of $\angle A$? _____

6. $\angle ABE$ and $\angle AEB$ have equal measures. What

   is the measure of each angle? _____

7. What is the measure of $\angle CBD$? _____

8. On Saturday, Clara started hiking at 10:00 A.M. and reached Clover Point at 12:40 P.M. She hiked at an average rate of

   3 miles per hour. How far did she go?_____

MIXED REVIEW

Find the product or quotient. Write the answer in simplest form.

1. $\frac{2}{3} \times \frac{1}{3}$ _____

2. $10 \times 3\frac{1}{2}$ _____

3. $\frac{2}{3} \div \frac{5}{6}$ _____

4. $1\frac{3}{7} \div \frac{2}{7}$ _____

Ratios

Write two equivalent fractions for the given ratio.

1. $\frac{5}{25}$ _____

2. $\frac{3}{6}$ _____

3. $\frac{14}{35}$ _____

4. $\frac{12}{16}$ _____

5. $\frac{9}{27}$ _____

6. $\frac{50}{60}$ _____

Write two ratios in three different ways for each diagram.

7. ▢ ▢ ▢
△ △ △ △ △   _____

8. ▢ ▢ ▢ ▢
◯ ◯ ◯ ◯ ◯
◯ ◯ ◯   _____

Write each ratio in two other ways.

9. $\frac{20}{36}$ _____

10. 6 to 7 _____

11. 3:8 _____

12. 8 to 3 _____

13. 12:7 _____

14. $\frac{10}{25}$ _____

Rewrite each ratio as a fraction in simplest form.

15. 15 to 18 _____

16. $\frac{20}{45}$ _____

17. 14:28 _____

18. $\frac{10}{14}$ _____

19. 25 to 45 _____

20. 24:80 _____

Mixed Applications

21. If there are 15 cats on the 3500 block of Pagosa St., about how many dogs are there?

_____

Ratio of Cats to Dogs on Pagosa St.

22. A dog can run $1\frac{1}{2}$ times as fast as a cat. If a cat can run 20 mph, how fast can a dog run?

_____

NUMBER SENSE

23. Which ratio does not belong in the group?

$\frac{4}{10}$, $\frac{15}{60}$, $\frac{6}{15}$, $\frac{24}{60}$ _____

60

Rates

Write a ratio in fraction form for each rate. Use equivalent fractions to solve.

1. 15 yd for 5 dresses
   ■ yd for 2 dresses

   _____

2. 42 days in 6 wk
   14 days in ■ wk

   _____

3. 16 eggs for 4 omelets
   ■ eggs for 2 omelets

   _____

4. 6 mi in 30 min
   8 mi in ■ min

   _____

5. $50 for 2 classes
   $■ for 3 classes

   _____

6. 150 km in 2 hr
   ■ km in 1 hr

   _____

Write the unit rate in fraction form.

7. 690 mi in 3 days

   _____

8. $300 in 20 days

   _____

9. 600 flowers/30 bouquets

   _____

10. 360 beads/12 necklaces

    _____

11. $54 in 9 hr

    _____

12. 336 mi/12 gal

    _____

13. 258 km/3 hr

    _____

14. $2.66/7 L

    _____

15. 232 mi in 16 hr

    _____

Mixed Applications

16. Tera can jog 5.5 mi in one hour. At the same rate, how far can she jog in 2 hours?

    _____

17. Joe can jog 6 mi in one hour. How much farther than Tera can he jog in 2 hours?

    _____

WRITER'S CORNER

18. Write a word problem to fit the following rates: 72 tokens/12 games,   ■ tokens/10 games.

    _____

    _____

Exploring Proportions

Compare the number of light cubes to the number of dark cubes.

1. Write a ratio for the comparison.

   _____

2. Separate the light cubes into two equal
   sets. Put an equal number of dark
   cubes in each of the two sets. Write a
   ratio for the comparison of the light to
   the dark cubes in each set.

   _____

3. How are the two ratios related?

   _____

4. Write a proportion to show the comparison of the two ratios. _____

5. Compare the cross products of the two ratios. _____

Look at these squares and circles.
Write a ratio in fraction form for each
of the following comparisons.

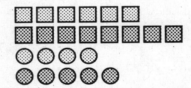

6. light squares to dark squares _____

7. light squares to light circles _____

8. dark squares to light squares _____

9. light circles to light squares _____

10. dark circles to light circles _____

11. dark circles to dark squares _____

VISUAL THINKING

12. Look at the diagram. Write a ratio in fraction form for the
    comparison of triangles to rectangles. (HINT: Remember
    to count triangles and rectangles of all sizes.)

    _____

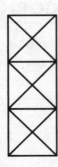

Solving Proportions

Solve each proportion.

1. $\frac{2}{18} = \frac{x}{36}$ _____

2. $\frac{7}{9} = \frac{63}{c}$ _____

3. $\frac{k}{3} = \frac{15}{18}$ _____

4. $\frac{7}{a} = \frac{14}{16}$ _____

5. $\frac{1}{4} = \frac{5}{y}$ _____

6. $\frac{h}{9} = \frac{64}{72}$ _____

7. $\frac{3}{5} = \frac{z}{20}$ _____

8. $\frac{d}{9} = \frac{4}{18}$ _____

9. $\frac{3}{c} = \frac{18}{30}$ _____

10. $\frac{5}{n} = \frac{25}{45}$ _____

11. $\frac{7}{8} = \frac{21}{b}$ _____

12. $\frac{15}{12} = \frac{e}{4}$ _____

Find the value of n.

13. $4:5 = n:20$ _____

14. 7 to 6 = n to 18 _____

15. $n:45 = 10:15$ _____

16. 5 to 25 = 1 to n _____

17. $8:36 = 2:n$ _____

18. n to 40 = 3 to 8 _____

19. $3:n = 6:15$ _____

20. 10 to n = 5 to 6 _____

Solve each proportion for x. Let a = 4, b = 3, and c = 2.

21. $\frac{a}{x} = \frac{b}{c}$ _____

22. $\frac{2c}{3a} = \frac{b}{x}$ _____

23. $\frac{a + 3b}{2c} = \frac{x}{ab}$ _____

Mixed Applications

24. Joan can paint 2 rooms of the same size in 5 hours. If she paints for $7\frac{1}{2}$ hours, how many rooms of the same size can she paint?

_____

25. The ratio of boys to girls in a science class is 8:7. If there are 14 girls, how many boys are in the class?

_____

LOGICAL REASONING

26. What fraction is equivalent to $\frac{4}{8}$ and has a numerator that is five less than three times the denominator?

_____

Problem-Solving Strategy
Use a Formula

Use a formula to solve.

1. A swimming pool is in the shape of a circle. The circumference is 6.594 m. What is the diameter?

_____

2. The circumference of a bike tire is 69.08 in. What is the diameter?

_____

3. The diameter of a can of corn is 77 mm. What is the circumference?

_____

4. The diameter of a basketball is 24 cm. What is the circumference?

_____

Mixed Applications	STRATEGIES	• Use a Formula • Work Backward • Solve a Simpler Problem • Find a Pattern

5. Scott makes monthly deposits to his savings account. During the past four months, he made the following deposits: $25, $30, $40, $60. If the pattern continues, how much will Scott deposit in the sixth month?

_____

6. Julia deposited $\frac{1}{2}$ of her paycheck in her savings account and $\frac{1}{4}$ of it in her checking account. She spent $22.76 of it on a T-shirt and then spent $\frac{1}{4}$ of what was left of her paycheck on lunch. When she arrived home, she had $16.68 of her paycheck left. How much money did Julia receive in her paycheck?

_____

7. Rita completed a 50-mile bike race in $2\frac{1}{4}$ hours. What was her average speed?

_____

8. The circumference of a highlight marker is about 21.98 mm. Find the diameter of the marker.

_____

SCIENCE CONNECTION

9. In a science experiment, flowers are blooming in a ratio of 1:2 from one day to the next. If on day 1 there are 5 flowers, how many flowers are there on day 3?

_____

Consumer Application
Unit Price

Use a proportion to find the unit price.

1. 5 for $1.55

_____

2. 4 for $1.76

_____

3. 9 for 54¢

_____

4. 12 for $13.32

_____

5. 11 for 99¢

_____

6. 7 for $1.61

_____

7. 4 for $5.00

_____

8. 5 for $67

_____

9. 3 for 96¢

_____

Find each unit price. Round to the next cent when necessary.
Then tell which choice has the lower unit price.

10. a 12-oz box of cereal for $2.55 or an 18-oz box of cereal for $3.29

_____

11. a 5-lb bag of grapefruit for $2.99 or an 8-lb bag of grapefruit for $5.25

_____

12. two paintbrushes for 59¢ or 5 paintbrushes for $1.29

_____

13. a package of 3 pairs of socks for $5.98 or a package of 8 pairs for $14.79

_____

Mixed Applications

14. Anne is shopping for notebooks. Which is the better buy?
3 for $3.29 or 2 for $2.89.

_____

15. About how long is the curved edge of $\frac{1}{4}$ of a 12-inch pizza? Round your answer to the nearest tenth of an inch.

_____

EVERYDAY MATH CONNECTION

16. Jeremy bought the following groceries:
5 lb of apples for $1.89, 8 lb of grapefruit for $4.88, 5 lb of potatoes for $0.99, and a 12-oz head of lettuce for 89¢.
What is the unit price for each item?

apples: _____   grapefruit: _____   potatoes: _____   lettuce: _____

Using Proportions
Similar Figures

Each pair of figures is similar. Find *x*.

1.

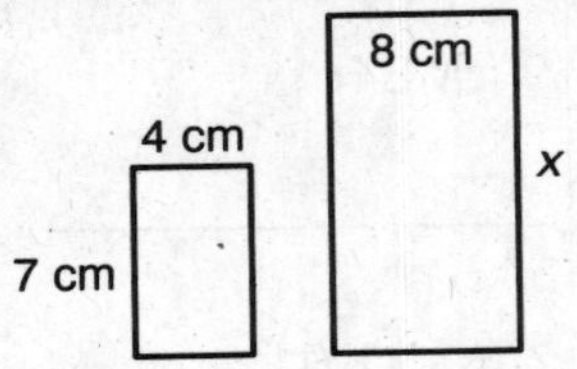

8 cm
4 cm
x
7 cm

____

2.

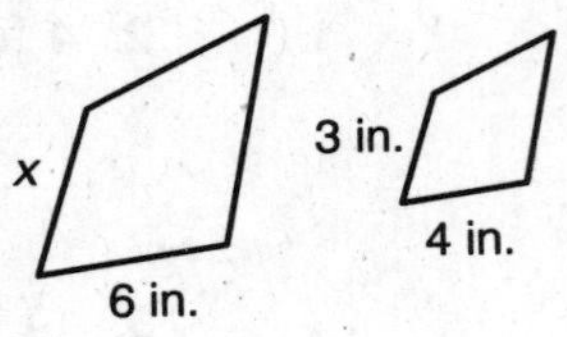

x
3 in.
4 in.
6 in.

____

3.

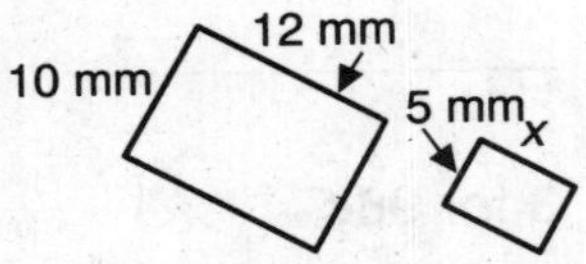

12 mm
10 mm
5 mm
x

____

4.

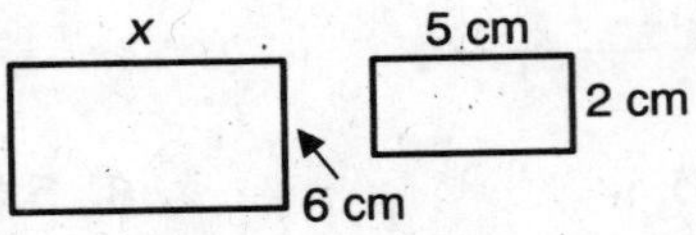

x
5 cm
2 cm
6 cm

____

5.

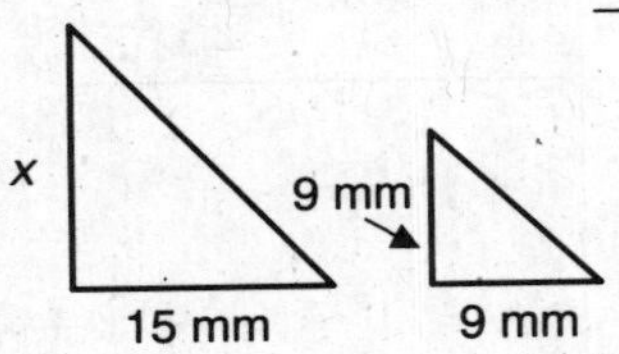

x
9 mm
15 mm
9 mm

____

6.

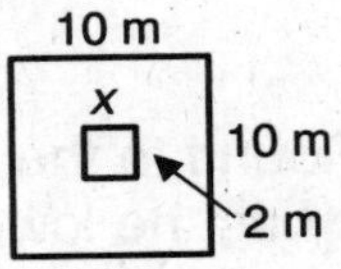

10 m
x
10 m
2 m

____

7.

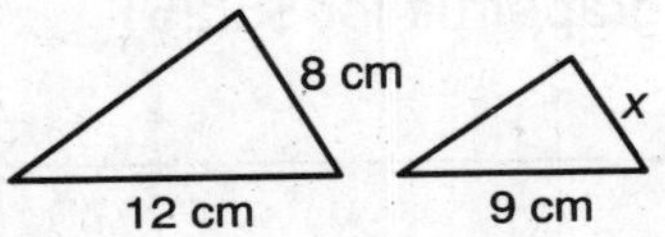

8 cm
x
12 cm
9 cm

____

8.

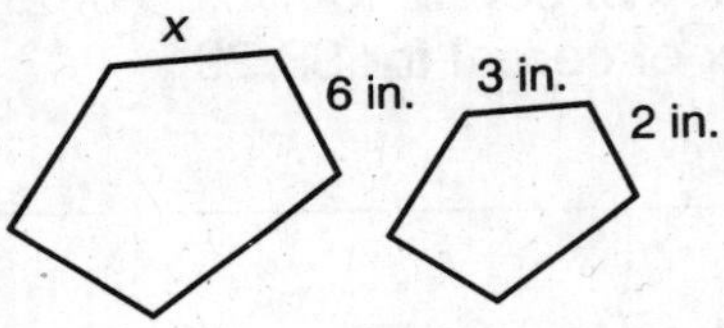

x
6 in.
3 in.
2 in.

____

Mixed Applications

9. The length and width of a rectangular box are 10 in. and 8 in., respectively. Another rectangular box has a length of 15 in. and a width of 12 in. respectively. Are the length and width dimensions of the two rectangular boxes similar?

____

10. Mrs. Nahamura bought 2.5 lb of fish filets for $5.50. What was the unit price of the fish filets?

____

MIXED REVIEW

Estimate.

1. $\frac{5}{6} + 1\frac{6}{7}$ _______________

2. $2\frac{3}{5} - 1\frac{1}{2}$ _______________

3. $\frac{4}{5} \times 39$ _______________

4. $15\frac{1}{8} \div 3\frac{1}{4}$ _______________

Application
Indirect Measurement

Each pair of triangles is similar. Find *x*.

1.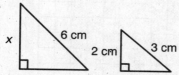

_____

2.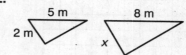

_____

3.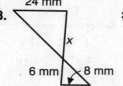

_____

4.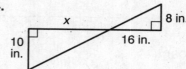

_____

5.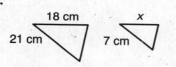

_____

6.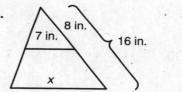

_____

Mixed Applications

7. A building casts a shadow that is 32 ft long at the same time a person 6 ft tall walking in front of the building casts an 8 ft shadow. What is the height of the building?

_____

8. Miyo has $1.25 in dimes and quarters. If one of the dimes were a quarter, she would have $1.40. How many dimes and how many quarters does Miyo have?

_____

NUMBER SENSE • MENTAL MATH

9. The sides of two triangles are in the ratio of 2:1. If the length of the sides of the first triangle are 5 cm, 9 cm, and 11 cm, what are the lengths of the sides of the second triangle?

_____

10. If the ratio of the triangles in Exercise 9 is reversed to 1:2, what will be the lengths of the sides of the second triangle?

_____

Introduction to Percent

Write a fraction, a decimal, and a percent for each shaded region.

1.

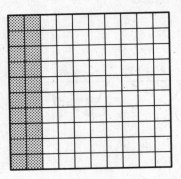

_____

2.

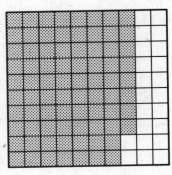

_____

Write as a percent.

3. $\frac{29}{100}$

_____

4. 2 out of 100

_____

5. $\frac{75}{100}$

_____

6. 95 out of 100

_____

7. $\frac{37}{100}$

_____

8. 0.11

_____

Mixed Applications

9. Larry is correct 54% of the time in his weather prediction. Express this percent as a fraction and as a decimal.

_____

10. Tomatoes are on sale for 3 lb for $1.09. How much will 5 lb of tomatoes cost?

_____

VISUAL THINKING

11. Look at the grids. What percent of each grid is shaded?

_____

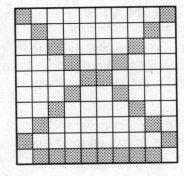 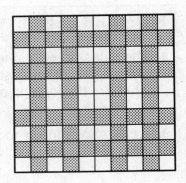

Connecting Percents and Decimals

Write each percent as a decimal.

1. 85% _____

2. 3% _____

3. 95% _____

4. 17% _____

5. 68% _____

6. 16.2% _____

7. 4% _____

8. 155% _____

9. 50% _____

10. 71.5% _____

11. 88.8% _____

12. 103% _____

Write each decimal as a percent.

13. 0.06 _____

14. 0.78 _____

15. 1.43 _____

16. 0.607 _____

17. 0.52 _____

18. 0.11 _____

19. 1.09 _____

20. 1.406 _____

21. 1.65 _____

Write each expression as a decimal. Then write each decimal as a percent.

22. ten and twelve hundredths

_____

23. thirty-seven and eight tenths

_____

Mixed Applications

24. The sale price of a TV was 82% of the original amount. Write the percent as a decimal.

_____

25. Pedro travels 286 mi in 4 hr 24 min. At this rate, how far will Pedro travel in 5 hr 24 min?

_____

NUMBER SENSE

26. The quotient $\frac{5}{7} \div \frac{15}{28}$ is $\frac{4}{3}$. Use 5, 7, 15, and 28 to write two other fractions that have a quotient of $\frac{4}{3}$ and two fractions that have a quotient of $\frac{3}{4}$.

_____

Connecting Percents and Fractions

Write each percent as a whole number or as a fraction in simplest form.

1. 71% _____

2. 3% _____

3. 410% _____

4. 160% _____

5. 56% _____

6. 66% _____

7. 78% _____

8. 84% _____

9. 28% _____

Write each fraction as a percent.

10. $\frac{11}{100}$ _____

11. $\frac{3}{4}$ _____

12. $\frac{63}{100}$ _____

13. $\frac{7}{10}$ _____

14. $\frac{48}{25}$ _____

15. $\frac{97}{100}$ _____

16. $\frac{700}{1,000}$ _____

17. $\frac{5}{8}$ _____

18. $\frac{22}{25}$ _____

Mixed Applications

19. About $\frac{4}{5}$ of the volume of Earth's atmosphere is nitrogen. What percent is this?

_____

20. Nakano's Car Sales increased its sales of sedans by 18%. By what fraction did the company increase its sales?

_____

21. About 21% of Earth's atmosphere is oxygen. Write this percent as a fraction.

_____

22. About 0.03 of Earth's water is fresh water. What percent is this?

_____

MIXED REVIEW

Find the value of the expression.

1. $(2 \cdot 2 - 2) \div 2 + 2$ _____

2. $[(6 + 3) \div 3 - 2] \cdot 2$ _____

Evaluate the expression. Let $x = 2$ and $y = 4$.

3. $(3x + 2y) \div 2$ _____

4. $\frac{1}{3x(6 - y)}$ _____

Special Percents

Write each fraction as a percent.

1. $\frac{3}{5}$ _____

2. $\frac{7}{2}$ _____

3. $\frac{3}{200}$ _____

4. $4\frac{4}{5}$ _____

5. $2\frac{1}{2}$ _____

6. $2\frac{7}{25}$ _____

7. $\frac{7}{1,000}$ _____

8. $\frac{15}{10}$ _____

9. $\frac{3}{500}$ _____

Write each percent as a decimal.

10. 9% _____

11. 55% _____

12. $2\frac{1}{2}$% _____

13. 225.03% _____

14. 410.6% _____

15. 0.02% _____

16. 160% _____

17. 6.9% _____

18. $120\frac{1}{2}$% _____

Write each percent as a fraction.

19. $\frac{1}{8}$% _____

20. $\frac{3}{5}$% _____

21. $1\frac{3}{4}$% _____

22. 120% _____

23. 175% _____

24. 2.5% _____

25. 200% _____

26. $\frac{2}{25}$% _____

27. $\frac{3}{50}$% _____

Mixed Applications

28. The Clear Valley District's annual budget for 1991 increased by $\frac{65}{1,000}$ of the annual budget from 1990. Write this fraction as a percent.

_____

29. The school budget increased from $5,800,000 to $6,150,000. By how much did the school budget increase?

_____

LOGICAL REASONING

30. Jacob has three coins worth $0.60 in his pocket. Two coins are the same. What coins does he have?

_____

Percent of a Number

Find the percent of each number.

1. 6% of 20 _____

2. 85% of 150 _____

3. 25% of 60 _____

4. 75% of 96 _____

5. 56% of 120 _____

6. 45% of 84 _____

7. 30% of 45 _____

8. 70% of 148 _____

9. 2% of 63 _____

Solve.

10. What number is 14% of 70?

_____

11. What number is 81% of 40?

_____

12. 75% of 240 is what number?

_____

13. 200% of $35 is what amount?

_____

14. What number is 26% of 130?

_____

15. What number is 1.7% of 19?

_____

Mixed Applications

16. In 1965 a dress cost $30.00. Fifteen years later, the price had increased by 115%. How much more did it sell for fifteen years later?

_____

17. How much further does a bicycle tire with a 30-in. diameter roll in one revolution than a tire with a 21-in. diameter?

_____

BUSINESS CONNECTION

Stockbrokers charge a fee for handling the sale of stock for an investor. Assume that a broker's fee is 1.5% of the sale price. Find the amount that the investor receives. Round to the next cent when necessary.

18. sale of 20 shares of Doubletock Publishing at $24 per share

_____

19. sale of 50 shares of Angel Air at 10\frac{1}{2}$ per share

_____

Problem Solving
Use a Graph

Janelle made a graph to show how she spends her yearly earnings. Suppose her yearly income is $24,000. Use the graph at the right to answer Exercises 1–7.

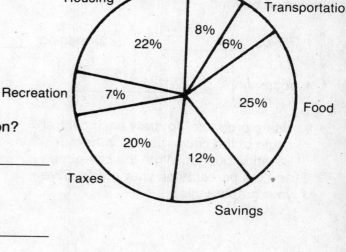

How much money does Janelle budget for

1. insurance?

   _____

2. transportation?

   _____

3. food?

   _____

4. housing?

   _____

5. recreation?

   _____

6. taxes?

   _____

7. savings?

   _____

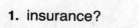 **Mixed Applications** → **STRATEGIES**   • Use a Graph • Use a Formula • Use Estimation • Guess and Check

Choose a strategy and solve.

8. Marta pays 28% of her $32,000 salary for rent. What does she pay for rent?

   _____

9. Marta saved $2,560 last year. What percentage of her salary is that?

   _____

10. Ginna jogged 7 mi in $1\frac{1}{2}$ hr. At what rate did Ginna jog?

   _____

11. The sum of two numbers is 68. Their difference is 16. What are the numbers?

   _____

NUMBER SENSE

12. In the number sequence below, insert one addition sign, one subtraction sign, and three decimal points to make a true statement.

    9 8 7 6 5 4 3 2 1 = 654% _____

73

Make a Circle Graph

The Johnsons made the following vacation budget: meals, 30%; lodging, 25%; transportation, 20%; recreation, 15%; other, 10%. Find the central angle measures for the Johnsons' vacation budget.

1. meals _____

2. lodging _____

3. transportation _____

4. recreation _____

5. other _____

6. Use a protractor to draw each central angle of the circle graph for the vacation budget. Write the categories and the percents on your graph. Give your graph a title.

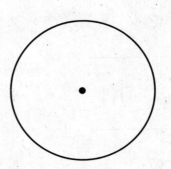

Mixed Applications

7. Suppose the Johnsons spent $900 on their vacation. Complete the table to show the amount that should be spent on each category.

Item	Percent	Amount
Meals		
Lodging		
Transportation		
Recreation		
Other		

8. At Columbo's concert, 40% of the people attending the concert were adult, 25% high school students, 15% middle school students, and 20% children younger than middle school age. Draw a circle graph that shows the percent of people in each category.

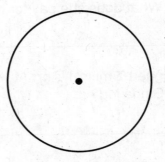

MIXED REVIEW

Find the value.

1. $12.4 - 6.113$ _____

2. $(1.5)^3$ _____

3. $(16.62)^0$ _____

Consumer Applications of Percent

Find the amount of discount at 30% off. Round to the nearest cent when necessary.

1. $7.00 _____ **2.** $110.50 _____ **3.** $99.00 _____

4. $65.00 _____ **5.** $78.50 _____ **6.** $240.00 _____

Find the amount of sales tax if the rate is 6%. Round to the nearest cent when necessary.

7. $8.00 _____ **8.** $112.50 _____ **9.** $92.00 _____

10. $65.00 _____ **11.** $80.25 _____ **12.** $235.00 _____

Find the sale price at 15% off. Round to the nearest cent when necessary.

13. $80.00 _____ **14.** $24.50 _____ **15.** $295.00 _____

16. $52.75 _____ **17.** $18.00 _____ **18.** $500.00 _____

Find the total cost if the sales tax rate is 7%. Round to the nearest cent when necessary.

19. $12.00 _____ **20.** $8.95 _____ **21.** $15.50 _____

Mixed Applications

22. Glowmart marked down their stock 32%. What will be the sale price of a $60 jacket?

_____

23. What is the total cost of a $28 pair of jeans if the sales tax is 7.5%?

_____

WRITER'S CORNER

24. Write and solve a word problem involving a $145.00 price and a 5.5% sales tax.

_____

Exploring Percent Problems

Use two-color counters to model each type of percent problem.

1. Line up 10 counters so all of them show blue. You want to turn over 40% of them to show red. Write a proportion to determine the number of red counters.
   Think: 40 is to 100 as what number is to 10?

   _____

2. Line up 10 counters so that 3 show blue and 7 show red. Write an equation to determine what percent are red.
   Think: What percent of 10 is 7?

   _____

3. Line up only 4 of the counters. Move the remaining 6 to the side. The 4 counters represent 40% of the total counters. Write an equation to determine the total number of counters.
   Think: 40% of what number is 4?

   _____

Choose the correct equation or proportion for each problem.
Circle a, b, or c.

4. Of 32 cars, 8 were sold. What percent were sold?

   a. $n\% \times 8 = 32$ **b.** $n\% \times 32 = 8$ **c.** $n = 8\%$ of 32.

5. Ryan is saving 40% of his allowance. Each week he receives $5. How much does he save each week?

   a. $\dfrac{40}{100} = \dfrac{n}{5}$ **b.** $\dfrac{40}{n} = \dfrac{5}{100}$ **c.** $\dfrac{40}{100} = \dfrac{5}{n}$

6. Maria sold 21 items. This is 30% of the total number she needs to sell. How many items must Maria sell?

   a. $21 \times n = 30\%$ **b.** $n = 30\% \times 21$ **c.** $30\% \times n = 21$

NUMBER SENSE

7. Out of 250 items for sale, 25 are marked down. What percent

   of the items are not marked down? _____

Finding the Percent One Number Is of Another

Solve. You may use either the proportion method or the equation method.

1. What percent of 55 is 22?

   _____

2. What percent of 48 is 12?

   _____

3. 17 is what percent of 50?

   _____

4. 18 is what percent of 60?

   _____

5. What percent of 50 is 34?

   _____

6. What percent of 25 is 18?

   _____

7. 15 is what percent of 75?

   _____

8. 30 is what percent of 60?

   _____

9. What percent of 45 is 25?

   _____

10. What percent of 75 is 45?

   _____

11. 30 is what percent of 120?

   _____

12. 18 is what percent of 90?

   _____

Mixed Applications

13. Joe earned $2,400 this year. Last year he earned $1,800. This year's earnings were what percentage of last year's?

   _____

14. Dolores bought 3 tapes that cost 4.95 each. The tax on her purchase was 6%. What was her total bill?

   _____

MIXED REVIEW

Solve the equation. Check your solution.

1. $x + 3.1 = 5$ _____

2. $0.9z = 10.8$ _____

3. $c - 0.34 = 2.19$ _____

4. $\frac{b}{0.05} = 5.3$ _____

Finding a Number When a Percent of It Is Known

Solve. You may use either the proportion method or the equation method.

1. 40% of what number is 16?

_____

2. 15% of what number is 75?

_____

3. 8 is 20% of what number?

_____

4. 18 is 9% of what number?

_____

5. 25% of what number is 14?

_____

6. 9% of what number is 54?

_____

7. 6 is 50% of what number?

_____

8. 67 is 67% of what number?

_____

9. 270 is 54% of what number?

_____

10. 2% of what number is 32?

_____

Mixed Applications

11. Casey earned $14,760 this year. This year's salary is 123% of last year's salary. How much did he earn last year?

_____

12. Aretha figured a 15% tip on a $5.40 lunch bill. She rounded the tip up to the next multiple of 5¢. What was the amount of Aretha's tip?

_____

BUSINESS CONNECTION

Many stores sell items at a percentage discount (discount rate). The sale price is the original price minus the discount. Find the discount and the sale price.

13. Original price: $15.50
Discount rate: 10%

Discount _____

Sale price _____

14. Original price: $32.00
Discount rate: 50%

Discount _____

Sale price _____

Estimating Percents

Choose the best estimate. Circle **a, b,** or **c.**

1. 61% of 50
   a. 20
   b. 25
   c. 30

2. 31% of $89
   a. $10
   b. $20
   c. $30

3. 67% of 211
   a. 140
   b. 150
   c. 180

Estimate the percent.

4. $\frac{64}{124}$ _____

5. $\frac{7}{25}$ _____

6. $\frac{9}{32}$ _____

7. 6 out of 49 _____

8. 42 out of 117 _____

9. 21 out of 81 _____

10. $\frac{33}{60}$ _____

11. $\frac{79}{155}$ _____

12. $\frac{165}{320}$ _____

Estimate the number.

13. 51 is 25% of what number?

_____

14. 8 is 9% of what number?

_____

Mixed Applications

15. Juan paid $59.99 for a jacket that originally sold for $85.50. About what percent of the original price did he pay for the jacket?

_____

16. In a circle graph showing audience share for 5 different programs, the central angle for program A is 54°. What percent of the audience does program A have?

_____

17. Of an order of bracelets, 65, or 84% of the total, arrived. How many bracelets in all were ordered?

_____

NUMBER SENSE
---

18. Dawn bought a book at a 35% discount. She paid $18.20. What was the original price?

_____

Integers

Write the opposite for each integer.

1. ⁻98 _____   **2.** ⁻1 _____   **3.** 1,011 _____   **4.** ⁻15 _____

5. Draw a number line to show all the integers from ⁻7 to 7.

Write an integer for each situation.

6. a loss of 14 points

_____

7. fifteen years ago

_____

8. a savings of $27.00

_____

Give the value of each.

9. |⁻3.5| _____   **10.** |⁻78| _____   **11.** |21| _____

12. |4.2| _____   **13.** |⁻15| _____   **14.** |101| _____

Write *sometimes*, *always*, or *never*.

15. The opposite of a negative integer is a negative integer. _____

16. The absolute value of an integer is its distance from zero. _____

Mixed Applications

17. The temperature was 12°C. It rose by 2°C. What is the new temperature?

_____

18. Walt bought a $35 pair of tennis shoes at 30% off. What did Walt pay for the tennis shoes?

_____

MATH CONNECTION

Order the integers from least to greatest.

19. ⁻6, ⁻10, 2 _____   **20.** 4, ⁻1, 0 _____   **21.** 6, ⁻3, ⁻8 _____

Adding Integers

Use a number line to find the sum.

1. 4 + ⁻2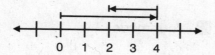

_____

2. ⁻5 + 1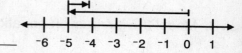

_____

3. ⁻8 + 8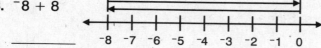

_____

4. ⁻6 + 3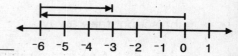

_____

5. 5 + ⁻6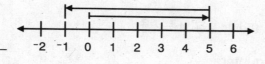

_____

6. 7 + ⁻8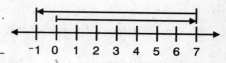

_____

Find the sum by using the absolute values.

7. 5 + 6 _____

8. ⁻16 + ⁻4 _____

9. 9 + ⁻9 _____

10. ⁻17 + ⁻8 _____

11. 24 + 30 _____

12. 8 + ⁻11 _____

13. 4 + 18 _____

14. 12 + ⁻2 _____

15. ⁻6 + 9 _____

16. ⁻8 + 2 _____

17. ⁻9 + ⁻1 _____

18. ⁻4 + 5 _____

19. 17 + 18 _____

20. ⁻7 + ⁻3 _____

21. 3 + ⁻9 _____

22. ⁻25 + ⁻2 + 49 _____

23. ⁻11 + |⁻2| _____

Mixed Applications

24. The temperature at 8 P.M. was ⁻8°C. By midnight, it had fallen two degrees. What was the temperature at midnight?

_____

25. Diana had $3\frac{1}{4}$ yd of material to make a shirt and a matching scarf. The shirt required $2\frac{2}{3}$ yd of the material. How much did she have left for the scarf?

_____

LOGICAL REASONING

26. If *a* and *b* are integers and *a* + *b* = 0, what do you know about the values of *a* and *b*?

_____

Exploring Integer Subtraction

Use red and blue counters to model equations.
Draw counters and complete.

1. Model the subtraction equation $^-2 - ^-4 = $ ■. Your model

   must have at least _____ red counters. To model the

   subtraction, take away _____ red counters. Since _____

   unpaired blue counters remain, $^-2 - ^-4 = $ _____ .

2. Use counters to model the addition equation $^-2 + 4 = $ ■.

   Since there are _____ blue unpaired counters,

   $^-2 + 4 = $ _____ .

3. Compare the subtraction equation with the addition

   equation. $^-2 - ^-4 = $ _____ and $^-2 + 4 = $ _____

   _____ = _____

Use counters to model and solve each subtraction equation.

4. $^-3 - ^-7 = $ _____

5. $^-3 - 7 = $ _____

6. $3 - ^-7 = $ _____

Rewrite each expression as an addition expression and solve.

7. $6 - 8$ _____

8. $^-8 - ^-6$ _____

9. $8 - ^-6$ _____

VISUAL THINKING

10. Let ⒝ represent 1 and ⓡ represent $^-1$.   ⒝⒝⒝⒝⒝⒝⒝⒝⒝
    Use the figure to solve $3 - 7$.   ⓡⓡⓡⓡⓡⓡⓡ

    _____

Subtracting Integers

Find the difference.

1. 13 − 9 _____

2. 0 − ⁻6 _____

3. 4 − 9 _____

4. 6 − ⁻9 _____

5. 14 − ⁻5 _____

6. 8 − ⁻6 _____

7. 0 − 7 _____

8. 12 − ⁻12 _____

9. ⁻9 − ⁻15 _____

10. ⁻6 − ⁻10 _____

11. 8 − 12 _____

12. ⁻15 − ⁻9 _____

13. 14 − 9 _____

14. ⁻17 − ⁻12 _____

15. ⁻9 − ⁻8 _____

16. ⁻11 − ⁻5 _____

17. ⁻13 − ⁻5 _____

18. ⁻6 − ⁻8 _____

19. ⁻15 − ⁻2 _____

20. 5 − 5 _____

21. ⁻8 − ⁻8 _____

Mixed Applications

22. The average temperature for the week of January 7–14 was ⁻16°C. The average temperature for the week of January 15–22 was 3°C. What is the difference between these two temperatures?

_____

23. Kareem bought a new collar and a toy mouse for his cat. The collar cost $3.50, the toy mouse cost $2.70, and the tax was 5%. How much change did Kareem get from a $10 bill?

_____

MATH CONNECTION

Find the difference. Use a calculator that has a [+/−] key.

Examples

A. 25 − 19
25 [−] 19 [=] [6   ]

B. 121 − 253
121 [−] 253 [=] [⁻132   ]

C. ⁻22 − 19
22 [+/−] [−] 19 [=] [⁻41   ]

D. ⁻88 − ⁻119
88 [+/−] [−] 119 [+/−] [=] [31   ]

24. 251 − 352 _____

25. 759 − 640 _____

26. 5,239 − 5,821 _____

27. 264 − 199 _____

Exploring Integer Multiplication

1. Complete the number line and integer addition to find
   $3 \times {}^-3 = \blacksquare$.

   $3 \times {}^-3 = {}^-3 + \underline{\hspace{1.2cm}} + \underline{\hspace{1.2cm}} = \underline{\hspace{1.5cm}}$

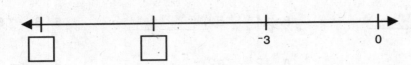

Complete the pattern.

2. $0 \times {}^-5 = 0$

   $1 \times {}^-5 = {}^-5$

   $2 \times {}^-5 = \underline{\hspace{1.2cm}}$

   $3 \times {}^-5 = \underline{\hspace{1.2cm}}$

   $4 \times {}^-5 = \underline{\hspace{1.2cm}}$

   $5 \times {}^-5 = \underline{\hspace{1.2cm}}$

3. ${}^-15 \times 3 = {}^-45$

   ${}^-12 \times 3 = {}^-36$

   ${}^-9 \times 3 = \underline{\hspace{1.2cm}}$

   ${}^-6 \times 3 = \underline{\hspace{1.2cm}}$

   ${}^-3 \times 3 = \underline{\hspace{1.2cm}}$

   $0 \times 3 = \underline{\hspace{1.2cm}}$

4. ${}^-1 \times {}^-3 = 3$

   ${}^-2 \times {}^-3 = \underline{\hspace{1.2cm}}$

   ${}^-3 \times {}^-3 = \underline{\hspace{1.2cm}}$

   ${}^-4 \times {}^-3 = \underline{\hspace{1.2cm}}$

   ${}^-5 \times {}^-3 = \underline{\hspace{1.2cm}}$

   ${}^-6 \times {}^-3 = \underline{\hspace{1.2cm}}$

Find the product.

5. ${}^-8 \times {}^-3$ \underline{\hspace{1.5cm}}

6. ${}^-8 \times 3$ \underline{\hspace{1.5cm}}

7. $8 \times {}^-3$ \underline{\hspace{1.5cm}}

8. ${}^-7 \times {}^-4$ \underline{\hspace{1.5cm}}

9. ${}^-7 \times 4$ \underline{\hspace{1.5cm}}

10. $7 \times {}^-4$ \underline{\hspace{1.5cm}}

Find the value.

11. $({}^-3)^3$ \underline{\hspace{1.5cm}}

12. $({}^-3)^1$ \underline{\hspace{1.5cm}}

13. $({}^-1)^2$ \underline{\hspace{1.5cm}}

14. $({}^-4)^2 = {}^-4 \times \underline{\hspace{1cm}} = \underline{\hspace{1cm}}$

15. $({}^-5)^3 = \underline{\hspace{1cm}} \times \underline{\hspace{1cm}} \times \underline{\hspace{1cm}} = \underline{\hspace{1cm}}$

LOGICAL REASONING

16. Write the next three numbers in the following pattern.

    ${}^-64, {}^-60, {}^-56, \underline{\hspace{1.5cm}}, \underline{\hspace{1.5cm}}, \underline{\hspace{1.5cm}}$

17. What are two ways to complete the pattern?

    \underline{\hspace{12cm}}

    \underline{\hspace{12cm}}

84

Dividing Integers

Find the quotient.

1. 14 ÷ 2 _____

2. 24 ÷ ⁻4 _____

3. ⁻36 ÷ 4 _____

4. ⁻27 ÷ 3 _____

5. ⁻18 ÷ ⁻2 _____

6. 121 ÷ ⁻11 _____

7. ⁻81 ÷ ⁻9 _____

8. 0 ÷ ⁻10 _____

9. 40 ÷ ⁻8 _____

10. ⁻105 ÷ 15 _____

11. 28 ÷ 7 _____

12. ⁻16 ÷ ⁻16 _____

13. 28 ÷ ⁻7 _____

14. ⁻32 ÷ ⁻4 _____

15. ⁻45 ÷ ⁻5 _____

16. ⁻82 ÷ ⁻41 _____

17. 25 ÷ ⁻5 _____

18. ⁻144 ÷ ⁻4 _____

19. 15 ÷ ⁻3 _____

20. ⁻32 ÷ 16 _____

21. ⁻100 ÷ ⁻25 _____

Mixed Applications

22. The temperatures for December 9–12 were ⁻12°C, ⁻6°C, 3°C, and 5°C. What is the average temperature for the four-day period?

_____

23. Computers and calculators are being sold at 25% off. Chante buys a calculator that is regularly priced at $75. How much does she pay?

_____

24. Heidi lost an average of 4 pounds a month for 5 months. What was her total weight loss?

_____

25. A car that has been getting 15 miles to a gallon of gas had a tune-up. Now it gets 18 miles a gallon. What is the percent of increase?

_____

MIXED REVIEW

Find the complement and the supplement for the angle with the given measure.

1. 8° _____

2. 36° _____

3. 89° _____

4. 41° _____

5. 65° _____

6. 73° _____

Properties of Integers

Name the properties that are used.

1. $4 \cdot {}^-13 = (4 \cdot {}^-8) + (4 \cdot {}^-5) = {}^-32 + {}^-20 = {}^-52$

   _____

2. $(7 + {}^-18) + 13 = ({}^-18 + 7) + 13 = {}^-18 + (7 + 13) = {}^-18 + 20 = 2$

   _____

3. $3 \cdot ({}^-4 \cdot {}^-6) = (3 \cdot {}^-4) \cdot {}^-6 = ({}^-12) \cdot {}^-6 = 72$

   _____

Complete.

4. $^-6 + 4 = 4 +$ _____ .

5. $^-16 + 16 = 16 +$ _____

6. $^-10 +$ _____ $= {}^-10$

7. _____ $\cdot {}^-15 = {}^-15$

8. _____ $\cdot 10 = {}^-10$

9. $8 \cdot {}^-5 = {}^-5 \cdot$ _____

10. $^-13 \cdot {}^-3 = {}^-3 \cdot$ _____

11. $^-23 \cdot {}^-14 = {}^-14 \cdot$ _____

12. $2 + ({}^-2 + 6) = ($ _____ $+ {}^-2) + 6$

13. $({}^-7 + {}^-6) + 3 = {}^-7 + ($ _____ $+ 3)$

14. $^-3 \cdot (4 + {}^-5) =$ _____ $+$ _____ $=$ _____

Mixed Applications

15. Bret's uncle is 54 years old. That is three times as old as the sum of the ages of Bret and his brother. Bret is twice as old as his brother. How old is Bret?

    _____

16. Angela spent $\frac{1}{3}$ of her money on a book and $\frac{2}{3}$ of it on a picture. If the book cost $11, how much money did she have to spend?

    _____

NUMBER SENSE

17. The sum of two integers is $^-5$. Their product is $^-24$. What are the integers?

    _____

Using Integers in Expressions

Write an expression for each.

1. seven less than a number, x

_____

2. six times a number, c

_____

3. a number, n, increased by 12

_____

4. a number, z, divided by 13

_____

Evaluate. Let $m = {}^-3$, $n = {}^-1$, and $p = {}^-12$.

5. $p + 10$ _____

6. ^-3n _____

7. $4m + 15$ _____

8. $\frac{p}{3}$ _____

9. $6n + m$ _____

10. $\frac{p}{m} + 3n$ _____

11. $n - p$ _____

12. $p - 4m$ _____

13. $m + \frac{p}{6}$ _____

Mixed Applications

14. Joe Grayelk invested $5,000 at 7.5% for 3 years. How much money did he have at the end of 3 years?

_____

15. The number of students who attended the spring play was four more than three times the number of adults. Write an expression to find the number of students attending the play.

_____

MIXED REVIEW

Name each triangle according to the measure of its angles.

1. 56°, 63°, 61°

_____

2. 35°, 55°, 90°

_____

3. 20°, 32°, 138°

_____

Classify each triangle according to the lengths of its sides.

4. 7 cm, 11 cm, 6 cm

_____

5. 4 in., 4 in., 4 in.

_____

6. 15 cm, 12 cm, 12 cm

_____

Using Integers to Solve Equations

Write what you would do to each side of the equation to solve.

1. $x - {}^-5 = 7$

_____

2. $n + 5 = {}^-2$

_____

3. $3w = {}^-27$

_____

4. $^-8t = {}^-120$

_____

5. $z \div 3 = {}^-3$

_____

6. $r + {}^-6 = {}^-7$

_____

Solve.

7. $n - {}^-2 = 8$

_____

8. $x + {}^-7 = {}^-4$

_____

9. $y - 6 = {}^-18$

_____

10. $t + {}^-9 = 5$

_____

11. $6y = {}^-18$

_____

12. $^-4a = {}^-36$

_____

13. $^-7c = 56$

_____

14. $11y = 33$

_____

15. $9r = {}^-63$

_____

16. $^-300x = 900$

_____

17. $15z = {}^-105$

_____

18. $^-2100t = {}^-6300$

_____

Mixed Applications

19. The attendance at the Jazz Festival has decreased by 74 people each year for the last 3 years. How many fewer people attend the festival this year than attended 3 years ago?

_____

20. Three times a number minus 2 is 25. What is the number?

_____

LOGICAL REASONING

21. Carlos rode the elevator up 4 floors, then down 2 floors. He then rode down 5 more floors and got off on the first floor. Where was Carlos when he began his elevator ride?

_____

Graphing Ordered Pairs

Give the ordered pair for each point named.

1. A _____   2. B _____

3. C _____   4. D _____

Give the name of the point for each ordered pair.

5. ($^-$4,5) _____   6. (1,0) _____

7. (0,3) _____   8. ($^-$3,$^-$2) _____

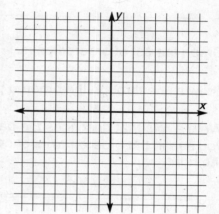

9. Graph the points for the ordered pairs.
   ($^-$3,2), (2,3), (4,0), ($^-$1,$^-$4)

10. Connect the points in Exercise 9 and
    name the figure.

_____

Mixed Applications

Use the figure you drew for Exercise 10.

11. Subtract 4 from each x-coordinate and
    5 from each y-coordinate. Give the new
    coordinates. Draw the new figure with
    the 4 new points.

    _____

    _____

12. Sue borrowed $14 dollars from Phil.
    She paid him $5. Write an addition
    sentence to show how much she still
    owes.

WRITER'S CORNER

13. Write a word problem about a rise or fall in temperature
    during a 12-hour period.

    _____

    _____

Exploring Linear Equations

1. Complete the table.

2. What pattern do you see for the value of *y* in each ordered pair?

   _____

3. State a rule to find the ordered pairs of the table.

   _____

4. Represent your rule with an equation.

   _____

x	y
⁻2	1
⁻1	2
0	3
1	☐
2	☐
3	☐

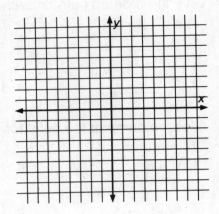

5. Graph the set of ordered pairs.

6. Draw a line through the ordered pairs.

7. Write a rule that describes the pattern you see in the ordered pairs shown at the right.

   _____

   _____

x	y
⁻2	⁻6
⁻1	⁻3
0	0
1	3
2	6

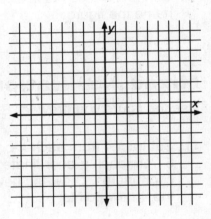

8. Write a linear equation for the rule you described in Exercise 7.

   _____

9. Graph the points that represent the ordered pairs in this table.

NUMBER SENSE

10. Write a linear equation for a graph that has the ordered pairs (⁻3,1), (1,1), and (3,1).

    _____

90

Number Sense
Other Names for Numbers

Give two other names for each number.

1. ⁻5

_____

2. 10.2

_____

3. 5.4%

_____

4. 6 out of 7

_____

5. 0.063

_____

6. $\frac{7}{100}$

_____

7. $\frac{11}{1,000}$

_____

8. 3 : 10

_____

Which number would be used for each situation?

9. cups of flour in a recipe for bread

    250% $2\frac{1}{2}$ $\frac{5}{2}$

_____

10. rate of sales tax

    5% $\frac{1}{20}$ $\frac{5}{100}$

Mixed Applications

11. Marilyn is in a secretarial pool. She works 5 days a week and earns $540 per week if she types 48 pages per day. How much is she paid per page?

_____

12. Greg purchased 17.5 gallons of gas, a sandwich for $2.25, and a magazine for $1.50. He spent a total of $24.24. What was the cost of the gasoline per gallon?

_____

MIXED REVIEW

Write the unit rate in fraction form.

1. 2 miles in $\frac{1}{2}$-hr

_____

2. 22 km in 2 hr

_____

3. 4 cm per $\frac{1}{4}$-min

_____

Solve each proportion.

4. $\frac{3}{8} = \frac{n}{24}$ _____

5. $\frac{x}{25} = \frac{7}{10}$ _____

6. $\frac{2}{3} = \frac{24}{y}$ _____

Terminating Decimals

Change each fraction to a terminating decimal. You may wish to use a calculator.

1. $\frac{3}{20}$ _____

2. $\frac{49}{50}$ _____

3. $\frac{9}{4}$ _____

4. $\frac{13}{20}$ _____

5. $\frac{13}{5}$ _____

6. $\frac{42}{1,000}$ _____

7. $\frac{31}{50}$ _____

8. $\frac{6}{25}$ _____

Write each terminating decimal as a mixed number or a fraction in simplest form.

9. 0.32 _____

10. 0.75 _____

11. 3.6 _____

12. 0.89 _____

13. 0.635 _____

14. 0.22 _____

15. 0.35 _____

16. 2.3 _____

Mixed Applications

17. Chiyo spends $\frac{7}{12}$ of an hour practicing the saxophone and 0.60 of an hour practicing the piano. Which instrument does she practice the most?

_____

18. The Minkowsi family is on a summer vacation. By noon one day, they had traveled 132 miles. By evening, they had traveled 352 miles. What fraction of the day's travel had they completed by noon?

_____

19. The librarian at Chester's public library noted that 25% of the books children borrowed on Friday were mystery stories, 12% were adventure tales, and the rest were nonfiction books. What fraction of the books borrowed by children were nonfiction?

_____

20. Steve is drawing a floor plan of his apartment using a scale of 0.5 cm = 1 ft. If his living room measures $20\frac{3}{4}$ ft long and $16\frac{1}{2}$ ft wide, what measurements should he give the living room on the floor plan?

_____

NUMBER SENSE

Use mental math and the fact that $\frac{1}{8}$ = 12.5% to express each fraction as a percent.

21. $\frac{1}{16}$ _____

22. $\frac{5}{16}$ _____

23. $\frac{7}{16}$ _____

Repeating Decimals

1. Use a calculator to find $\frac{1}{9}$.

$1 \div 9 = \boxed{\textbf{0.1111111}}$

$\frac{1}{9} = $ _____ $= $ _____

Use $\frac{1}{9} = 0.\overline{1}$ to find each fraction as a decimal.

2. $\frac{2}{9} = $ _____   3. $\frac{5}{9} = $ _____   4. $\frac{10}{9} = $ _____   5. $\frac{1}{45} = $ _____

Rewrite each repeating decimal. Use a bar to indicate repeating digits.

6. 0.263263 . . . _____   7. 0.3812441244 . . . _____

8. 0.113113 . . . _____   9. 3.1298319831 . . . _____

Use a calculator to express each fraction as a decimal. Use a bar to indicate repeating digits.

10. $\frac{5}{12}$ _____   11. $\frac{5}{3}$ _____   12. $\frac{8}{3}$ _____   13. $\frac{22}{9}$ _____

14. $\frac{10}{9}$ _____   15. $\frac{7}{12}$ _____   16. $\frac{4}{11}$ _____   17. $\frac{7}{18}$ _____

Express each fraction as a decimal. Use the values $\frac{1}{3} = 0.\overline{3}$ and $\frac{1}{9} = 0.\overline{1}$.

18. $\frac{10}{3}$ _____   19. $\frac{11}{9}$ _____   20. $\frac{1}{90}$ _____

LOGICAL REASONING

21. Use $\frac{2}{3} = 0.6666 \ldots = 0.\overline{6}$ to mentally find $\frac{2}{27}$, $\frac{4}{27}$, and $\frac{8}{27}$.
    Then find a pattern and express as a decimal: $\frac{10}{27}$, $\frac{20}{27}$, and $\frac{80}{27}$.

    _____

Exploring Rational Numbers

Predict whether each fraction can be changed to a terminating or a repeating decimal. Then use a calculator to find the decimal.

1. $\frac{17}{80}$ _____

   $17 \div 80 =$ ▢

2. $\frac{25}{32}$ _____

   $25 \div 32 =$ ▢

3. $\frac{19}{48}$ _____

   $19 \div 48 =$ ▢

Write each rational number as the ratio of two integers.

4. $^{-}2.2$ _____

5. $^{-}5$ _____

6. 2 _____

7. $5\frac{1}{8}$ _____

8. 22% _____

9. $0.\overline{7}$ _____

Predict whether the fraction can be changed to a terminating or a repeating decimal. Then write the decimal.

10. $\frac{5}{16}$ _____

    _____

11. $\frac{9}{250}$ _____

    _____

12. $\frac{3}{25}$ _____

    _____

13. $\frac{6}{11}$ _____

    _____

14. $\frac{5}{18}$ _____

    _____

15. $\frac{7}{15}$ _____

    _____

16. $\frac{11}{9}$ _____

    _____

17. $\frac{6}{33}$ _____

    _____

18. $\frac{3}{5}$ _____

    _____

VISUAL THINKING

19. Every rational number can be represented on a number line. Express each number identified by a letter as a ratio of two integers and as a decimal.

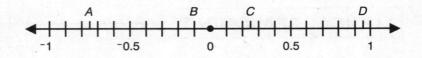

   a. point A _____

   b. point B _____

   c. point C _____

   d. point D _____

Comparing and Ordering Rational Numbers

Write the opposite of each rational number in the form $\frac{a}{b}$, where $b \neq 0$.

1. $^-12\frac{1}{2}$ _____

2. $8\frac{5}{8}$ _____

3. 13 _____

4. $^-0.13$ _____

5. $^-8.57$ _____

6. 10.63 _____

7. $^-26$ _____

8. 0.8 _____

Compare. Write <, >, or =.

9. $3\frac{5}{8} \bigcirc 3.6$

10. $^-6\frac{3}{25} \bigcirc {}^-6.15$

11. $\frac{11}{50} \bigcirc \frac{6}{25}$

12. $\frac{3}{16} \bigcirc \frac{2}{12}$

13. $4\frac{9}{20} \bigcirc 4\frac{1}{2}$

14. $^-81.6 \bigcirc {}^-81\frac{2}{3}$

15. $^-3\frac{3}{5} \bigcirc {}^-3.6$

16. $^-8.0 \bigcirc {}^-8\frac{1}{12}$

17. $^-16\frac{1}{2} \bigcirc 16\frac{1}{2}$

Write in order from least to greatest.

18. $^-5.8, {}^-7, 3\frac{5}{8}, 1\frac{2}{3}$

_____

19. $\frac{7}{9}, \frac{^-5}{12}, \frac{^-7}{32}, {}^-0.5, 1.1$

_____

Mixed Applications

20. Donelle and Connie measured the same piece of wood. Donelle measured it to be $25\frac{3}{16}$ in. Connie's measurement was 25.2 in. Which person's measurement was the greater by how much?

_____

_____

21. Amir put 40% of his money in a savings account. He spent $\frac{1}{3}$ of the remaining amount on film. After spending $4.56 on lunch, he had $11.44 left. How much money did Amir have in the beginning?

_____

_____

NUMBER SENSE

22. When $^-96$ is divided by an integer, the quotient is $^-13$ and there is a remainder of $^-5$. What is the divisor?

_____

The Density Property

Name a rational number between the two numbers of each pair.

1. ⁻5 and ⁻6

_____

2. $\frac{5}{16}$ and 0.3

_____

3. $\frac{3}{8}$ and $\frac{5}{8}$

_____

4. 1.63 and 1.64

_____

5. $\frac{3}{5}$ and 0.7

_____

6. ⁻15.2 and ⁻15.3

_____

7. $\frac{7}{16}$ and $\frac{15}{32}$

_____

8. 2.500 and 2.550

_____

9. $\frac{4}{5}$ and $\frac{7}{8}$

_____

10. 1.94 and 1.95

_____

11. $1\frac{1}{5}$ and $1\frac{3}{10}$

_____

12. ⁻0.2 and $\frac{-3}{16}$

_____

13. 400.7 and 400.71

_____

14. 4.07 and 4.08

_____

15. $1\frac{3}{16}$ and 1.20

_____

Mixed Applications

16. A train traveling from Seattle to Denver averages 82.3 miles per hour. On the return trip, the average speed is 78.5 miles per hour. What is the average speed for the round trip?

_____

17. A precise measurement for a small opening is taken 4 times with the following readings: $8\frac{9}{50}$ mm, 8.19 mm, 8.20 mm and $8\frac{1}{5}$ mm. Find the average of the four readings.

_____

WRITER'S CORNER

18. Write a riddle about a mystery rational number. Give the reader at least two clues that will allow him or her to find the solution.

_____

_____

_____

Integers as Exponents

Extend the pattern for the powers of 10.

1. $10^4 = 10{,}000$

$10^5 = 100{,}000$

$10^6 = $ _____

$10^7 = $ _____

2. $10^{-2} = 0.01$

$10^{-3} = 0.001$

$10^{-4} = $ _____

$10^{-5} = $ _____

Complete.

3. $3^3 = 3 \times 3 \times 3 = 27$

$3^2 = $ _____ $= $ _____

$3^1 = $ _____ $= $ _____

$3^0 = $ _____ $= $ _____

4. $3^{-1} = \frac{1}{3^1} = \frac{1}{3}$

$3^{-2} = $ _____ $= $ _____

$3^{-3} = $ _____ $= $ _____

$3^{-4} = $ _____ $= $ _____

Rewrite each fraction, using a negative exponent.

5. $\frac{1}{10^5}$ _____

6. $\frac{1}{3^9}$ _____

7. $\frac{1}{10^{11}}$ _____

8. $\frac{1}{6^3}$ _____

Rewrite each expression, using a positive exponent.

9. 10^{-9} _____

10. 2^{-14} _____

11. 4^{-8} _____

12. 10^{-12} _____

Write each number, using a base of 10 and a negative exponent.

13. 0.00001 _____

14. 0.0000001 _____

MIXED REVIEW

The figures are similar. Find x.

1. 3 cm x 4 cm 2 cm _____

2. 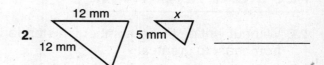 12 mm 12 mm 5 mm x _____

Find the unit price.

3. 8 for $2.56 _____

4. 25 for $14.00 _____

5. 6 for $13.14 _____

Scientific Notation

Complete the following.

1. $0.000095 = 9.5 \times$ _____

2. $0.000836 = 8.36 \times$ _____

3. _____ $\times 10^{-3} = 0.00705$

4. _____ $\times 10^{-5} = 0.00002119$

Write in scientific notation.

5. 0.0000364

6. 0.00751

7. 0.10005

8. $1{,}094$

9. 0.00000099

10. 0.04101

11. $10{,}500$

12. $8{,}900$

Write in standard form.

13. 7.4×10^{-4}

14. 8.3×10^{-2}

15. 1.95×10^{-3}

16. 2.8×10^{-5}

17. 5.45×10^{3}

18. 9.2×10^{5}

19. 6.091×10^{-4}

20. 9.09×10^{-1}

Mixed Applications

21. The speed of light is about 3×10^{5} kilometers per second. Write this speed in standard form.

22. How many seconds are there in one week? Write your answer in scientific notation.

LOGICAL REASONING

23. Without writing these numbers in standard form, order them from least to greatest.

$4.1 \times 10^{7} \qquad 3.62 \times 10^{-6} \qquad 4.1 \times 10^{-2} \qquad 3.62 \times 10^{-2} \qquad 4.1 \times 10^{9}$

Square Roots

Find the square or square root.

1. 15^2 _____   2. $\sqrt{64}$ _____   3. 10^2 _____   4. $^-\sqrt{25}$ _____

5. $\left(\frac{1}{4}\right)^2$ _____   6. $\sqrt{196}$ _____   7. $(2.11)^2$ _____   8. $^-\sqrt{\frac{1}{121}}$ _____

9. $\left(\frac{2}{9}\right)^2$ _____   10. $\sqrt{0.64}$ _____   11. $(^-8)^2$ _____   12. $\sqrt{0.0036}$ _____

Estimate each square root to the nearest tenth.

13. $\sqrt{24}$ _____   14. $\sqrt{73}$ _____   15. $\sqrt{146}$ _____   16. $\sqrt{5}$ _____

17. $\sqrt{101}$ _____   18. $\sqrt{61}$ _____   19. $\sqrt{300}$ _____   20. $\sqrt{486}$ _____

Use a calculator to find each square root. Round to the nearest tenth.

21. $\sqrt{21}$ _____   22. $\sqrt{56}$ _____   23. $\sqrt{13}$ _____   24. $\sqrt{91}$ _____

25. $\sqrt{110}$ _____   26. $\sqrt{87}$ _____   27. $\sqrt{250}$ _____   28. $\sqrt{17}$ _____

Mixed Applications

29. A square lot has an area of 160,000 square ft. What is the length of each side?

_____

30. A circle has a circumference of 35.2 cm. What is its diameter?

_____

31. What is the 6% sales tax on a computer that costs $4,200?

_____

32. A square room has a floor area of 410 m². What is the length of each side to the nearest tenth of a meter?

_____

NUMBER SENSE

33. You know that there are whole numbers between any two perfect squares greater than 0. Between which of these pairs of perfect squares are there more whole numbers? Answer without calculating.

   a. between 59^2 and 60^2 _____

   b. between 590^2 and 591^2 _____

Looking Beyond Rational Numbers

Classify each number as *rational* or *irrational*. Use a calculator if necessary.

1. 33

_____

2. $\sqrt{33}$

_____

3. $^-\sqrt{256}$

_____

4. $0.\overline{7}$

_____

5. $^-\frac{5}{16}$

_____

6. $\sqrt{3}$

_____

7. $0.\overline{899}$

_____

8. $\sqrt{111}$

_____

Complete the table. Classify each number by placing an X in each appropriate column.

		Real Number	Rational Number	Whole Number	Integer	Irrational Number
9.	$^-2$					
10.	4.2					
11.	$\sqrt{21}$					
12.	$0.\overline{8}$					
13.	$^-3.96213\ldots$					

Mixed Applications

14. A pattern for a dress needs $3\frac{1}{3}$ yd of fabric. If Mary buys $9\frac{1}{3}$ yd and $6\frac{3}{4}$ yd of fabric, will she have enough to make 5 dresses? Explain.

_____

_____

15. Kim has 196 floor tiles. Each tile is 1-ft square. Can he use all the floor tiles to make a square without cutting any of the tiles? Explain.

_____

_____

SCIENCE CONNECTION

16. The formula for a falling object is $S = 16t^2$, where S is the distance in feet and t is the time in seconds. About how long will it take an object to fall 96 ft?

_____

Problem-Solving Strategy
Use a Table

1. The table shows the number of people attending the convention since 1987. Use the table to predict the number of people attending the convention in 1992.

Year	Number of People (in hundreds)
1987	3
1988	5
1989	7
1990	9
1991	11

2. The amount Juanita still needs to save for a cassette player has decreased steadily since January. Use the table to predict the amount she still needs to save in July.

Month	Amount to Be Saved
January	$32
February	$31
March	$29
April	$26
May	$22

Mixed Applications > **STRATEGIES** • Use a Table • Work Backward • Write a Formula • Guess and Check

Choose a strategy and solve.

3. The table gives postage rates for first-class mail. Use the table to determine the cost of mailing a first-class letter weighing 10 ounces.

First Class

First ounce	29¢
Each additional ounce	23¢

4. During one week, Marco worked 5 hr more than twice the number of hours Michael worked. If Marco worked 29 hr in one week, how many hours did Michael work?

5. To go on a school field trip, each adult paid $15 and each student paid $12. A total of 20 people went on the trip and paid a total of $261. How many adults and how many students went on the field trip?

NUMBER SENSE

6. The square of a given number is the same as three times the number. What is the number?

Exploring Combinations

David ordered a subway sandwich. His choice of ingredients were: ham, turkey, roast beef, salami, lettuce, and pickles. How many different ways could David order a sandwich with 2 ingredients?

Mark 6 cards with the letters H, T, R, S, L, and P to represent the ingredients.

1. List all the different ways you can choose the second ingredient when H is the first ingredient. Use the form (H, T).

   _____

2. Repeat this process using each of the other choices for the first ingredient.

   _____

   _____

3. Since a sandwich with ham and cheese is the same as a sandwich with cheese and ham, cross out the pairs that reverse the pairs already listed. How many pairs remain in the list?

   _____

4. Use your cross-out pattern to find an addition sentence to show the number of combinations of 6 ingredients taken 2 at a time.

   _____

5. How many different 2-letter combinations can you make from the first 8 letters of the alphabet? Remember: (A, B)

   is the same as (B, A). _____

VISUAL THINKING

6. Mark 5 points around a circle. How many triangles can be drawn by connecting the points so that all the vertices of the triangles lie on the

   circle? _____

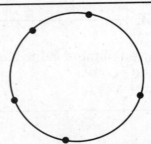

Exploring Permutations

John, Mary, Andrew, Chantelle, and Scott are seated in a row
of 5 seats. In how many different ways can they be seated? _____

Mark 5 cards J, M, A, C, and S to represent the 5 people.

1. How many choices of seats does the first person have? _____

2. How many seats are left for the second person? _____

3. How many seats are then left for the third person? _____

4. How many seats are then left for the fourth person? _____

5. How many seats remain for the fifth person? _____

6. Find the number of different arrangements of the 5 people.
   Could you do this by multiplying 5 × 4 × 3 × 2 × 1? Explain.

   _____

   _____

7. In how many ways can 7 students be
   seated at 7 desks?

   _____

8. In how many different ways can 6
   people line up in a lunch line?

   _____

9. There are 8 candidates running for the offices of president,
   vice-president, secretary, treasurer, and representative.
   How many different results could there be in the election?
   Remember, Person 1 being elected president is different from
   Person 1 being elected to another office.

   _____

NUMBER SENSE

The product 4 × 3 × 2 × 1 is a special product called "4 factorial."
It is symbolized by the expression 4! The value of 4! is 24.

Find the value of these factorial expressions.

10. 5! _____ 11. 6! _____ 12. 7! _____ 13. 9! _____

Introduction to Chance Events

Use this information for Exercises 1–6.

Marcia draws one coin from a container to
help her decide where she will go to dinner.
In the container are 4 pennies, 4 nickels,
2 dimes, and 3 quarters.

Coins	Outcomes
Penny	Dinner at a fast-food restaurant
Nickel	Dinner at a family restaurant
Dime	Dinner at a fancy restaurant
Quarter	Dinner at home

Are the outcomes in each pair likely?

1. Dinner at a fast-food restaurant. Dinner
   at a family restaurant.

   _____

2. Dinner at home. Dinner at a fancy
   restaurant.

   _____

3. Dinner at a fast-food restaurant. Dinner
   at home.

   _____

4. Dinner at a fancy restaurant. Dinner
   at home.

   _____

Write whether each event is *certain, impossible,* or *neither.*

5. Marcia goes out to dinner.

   _____

6. Marcia eats dinner.

   _____

Mixed Applications

7. In Marcia's coin container, what is the
   ratio of quarters to nickels?

   _____

8. What percent of Marcia's coins are
   worth 10¢ or more?

   _____

9. A jar has 6 marbles, 4 red and 2 blue.
   What is the ratio of blue to red marbles? _____

LOGICAL REASONING

10. What is wrong with this problem?

    The sum of each pair of numbers on opposite sides of a
    number cube (with dots 1 to 6) equals 6. Find the numbers
    that could be on each pair of opposite sides.

    _____

Probability of a Simple Event

Use the spinner and table for Exercises 1–9.

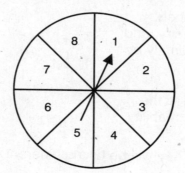

	Item	Color
1.	penny	red
2.	nickel	blue
3.	dime	green
4.	quarter	red
5.	2 dimes	red
6.	2 quarters	blue
7.	dollar	blue
8.	5 nickels	red

Write the probability of each event as a fraction in simplest form.

1. a penny _____

2. a quarter _____

3. at least 25¢ _____

4. at least 50¢ _____

5. at most 25¢ _____

6. at most 50¢ _____

7. red _____

8. blue _____

9. green _____

Mixed Applications

10. There are 10 sweaters in a drawer. Four of them are blue; 2 are green. In simplest form, write the probability of choosing a blue sweater.

11. In Exercise 10, what is the probability of choosing a green sweater?

_____

_____

WRITER'S CORNER

12. Choose five possible breakfast foods. Draw a spinner so that your favorite breakfast food has the greatest probability of being selected. Write a problem about the probability of selecting each breakfast item.

_____

_____

_____

Problem-Solving Strategy
Make an Organized List

Julia and Samuel are studying to be engineers. Five of their required courses are Algebra, Calculus, Physics, Chemistry, and Computer Programming. The courses are assigned randomly by a computer.

Organize a list of all possible ways they could be assigned the courses if they each take one course. Then find each probability.

1. Julia and Samuel will be taking the same course.

   _____

2. They will be taking different courses.

   _____

3. Neither one will be in Chemistry or Computer Programming.

   _____

4. Julia will be in either Algebra or Physics, and Samuel will be in either Calculus or Chemistry.

   _____

Mixed Applications	STRATEGIES	• Make an Organized List • Use a Formula • Guess and Check • Use Estimation

5. Clarisa left a 15% tip of $1.80 for a haircut. How much was the cost of the haircut without the tip?

   _____

6. Out of 8 candidates (A, B, C, D, E, F, G, H), 2 will be chosen Chairperson and Secretary of a committee. In how many ways can the two offices be filled?

   _____

WRITER'S CORNER

7. There are five movies being shown at the Value Theater. Write a problem about the probability of two or three people attending the same movie at the same time. Solve.

   _____

   _____

   _____

Exploring Experimental Probability

Use the spinner for Exercises 1–6.

You spin this spinner 10 times and land on blue 3 times.

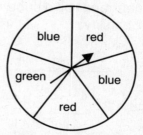

1. What is the experimental probability of landing on blue?

_____

2. List the possible outcomes for the spinner.

_____

3. What is the mathematical probability of landing on blue?

_____

4. Is the experimental probability of $\frac{3}{10}$ close to the mathematical probability of landing on blue? Explain.

_____

5. If you spin this spinner 50 times, would it be reasonable to land on blue 22 times? Explain.

_____

_____

6. You spin the spinner 500 times. Use mathematical probability to predict the number of times you will land on red.

_____

7. You will roll a cube numbered 1–6 30 times. Predict how many times it will show a 1.

_____

8. You will roll a number cube 50 times. Predict how many times it will land on an even number.

_____

9. You spin the spinner at the top of this page 20 times. Predict the number of times it will not land on red.

_____

10. You toss a coin 40 times. Predict how many times it will land on tails.

_____

EVERYDAY MATH CONNECTION

11. Shane is on a baseball team. He averages 6 hits in 30 times at bat. How many hits would you expect him to have after 180 times at bat? _____

Independent Events

Spin this spinner and roll a cube numbered 1–6 at the same time.
Find each probability.

1. red and a 6 _____

2. green and a 2 _____

3. blue and not 3 _____

4. yellow and an
   even number _____

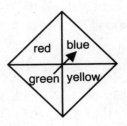

5. purple and a 4 _____

6. blue and a 7 _____

Roll the number cube two times. Find each probability.

7. a 1 and a 5 _____

8. a 2 and an odd number _____

9. an even number and a 1 _____

10. an even number
    and an odd number _____

Mixed Applications

A box contains 4 blue marbles, 5 red marbles, 2 green marbles
and 1 purple marble. You pick a marble at random, replace it, and
then pick another marble at random. Find each probability.

11. blue and red _____

12. green and purple _____

13. blue, blue, and red _____

14. blue and blue _____

MIXED REVIEW

Write a fraction for the percent. Solve.

1. 75% of 96

2. 42% of 100

3. 9% of 40

_____

_____

_____

Write a decimal for the percent. Solve.

4. 5% of 36

5. 12% of 500

6. $3\frac{1}{2}$% of 500

_____

_____

_____

Dependent Events

A box contains 4 white crayons, 3 red crayons, 3 blue crayons, and 2 purple crayons. You pick a crayon at random and then draw a second crayon without replacing the first. Find each probability.

1. P (white, then red) _____

2. P (red, then blue) _____

3. P (purple, then white) _____

4. P (white, then white) _____

5. P (red, then red) _____

6. P (blue, then blue) _____

7. P (purple, then purple) _____

8. P (red, then white) _____

9. P (purple, then black) _____

10. P (blue, then red) _____

Mixed Applications

11. Mimi's purse contains 5 quarters, 4 dimes, 4 nickels, and 2 pennies. Mimi draws one coin at random and then draws a second coin without replacing the first. Find the probability of drawing a quarter, then a dime.

_____

12. From Exercise 11, find the probability of drawing a quarter, then another quarter.

_____

13. Using Exercise 11, write a ratio for the chance of drawing a dime on the first draw and a nickel from the second draw.

_____

14. Sean has 10 black socks, 6 blue socks, and 2 brown socks in his drawer. He selects 1 sock and then another without replacing the first. What is the probability that he will select 2 black socks?

_____

NUMBER SENSE

15. How many different ratios can be made with the digits 1, 2, 4, 6, and 8? Write the ratio in fraction form. If the two ratios are equivalent, they are not different.

_____

Exploring Simulations

Use a large jar full of dried beans. Grab a handful of beans, count them, and mark a colored "x" on each bean. Put the marked beans back in the jar and mix all the beans together. Now grab another handful of beans.

1. Write a fraction to show the ratio of those marked "x" to the total number of beans in your new handful, or sample.

   _____

2. Now write a proportion to estimate the number of beans in the jar.

   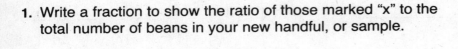

   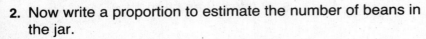

3. Let the handful of beans from the first handful represent the first sample of birds an ecology worker catches and marks. What does the x represent?

   _____

4. How would you use a table of 20 random digits containing digits 0 through 9 to simulate 100 spins of a 10-item spinner?

   _____

   _____

   _____

   _____

MIXED REVIEW

1. What percent of 25 is 10? _____

2. 25% of what number is 6? _____

3. What number is 15% of 40? _____

4. What percent of 36 is 18? _____

5. 384 is 32% of what number? _____

6. What number is $37\frac{1}{2}$% of 112? _____

Problem-Solving Strategy
Conduct a Simulation

At a company that makes soda cans, something went wrong with the machine that stamps the type of soda on the can. For about 3 hours, it stamped *orange drink* on cans of grape drink, it stamped *grape drink* on cans of cola, and it did not stamp some of the cans at all. The machine stamps about 1,500 cans per hour.

1. The plant foreman decides to run the machine for $\frac{1}{2}$ hr. What information can be gained from this trial run?

   _____

   _____

   _____

2. The plant foreman found that out of 750 cans stamped in the $\frac{1}{2}$-hr trial run, 150 were not stamped. About how many were not stamped in 3 hours?

   _____

3. Of the 750 cans in the trial run, 500 were incorrectly stamped *orange drink*. About how many cans were incorrectly stamped *orange drink* in 3 hours?

   _____

4. Use the information from Exercises 2 and 3. Suppose the remainder of the 750 cans were incorrectly stamped *grape drink*. About how many cans were incorrectly stamped *grape drink* in 3 hours?

   _____

Mixed Applications ➤ **STRATEGIES** • Make an Organized List • Draw a Design • Write an Equation • Conduct a Simulation

5. The label on a box is either right side up (R) or upside down (U). In how many different ways can the labels on a group of 8 boxes appear?

   _____

6. Use the information from Exercises 1–4. About how many cans were incorrectly stamped *orange drink* or *grape drink* in 2 hours?

   _____

LOGICAL REASONING

7. You spin 4 spinners independently. The probabilities of each spinner landing on 3 are $\frac{1}{8}$, $\frac{3}{6}$, $\frac{1}{4}$, and $\frac{3}{8}$, respectively.

   Find the probability of P (3, 3, 3, 3). _____

Precision of Measurement

Tell which measurement is more precise.

1. 30 oz or 2 lb   _____

2. $1\frac{1}{2}$ hr or 85 min   _____

3. 3.1 kg or 3.10 kg   _____

4. 5 cm or 53 mm   _____

5. 50 hr or 2 days   _____

6. 6.1 in. or 6 in.   _____

7. 17 yd or 50 ft   _____

8. 9 ft or 9.0 ft   _____

Write the letter of the most precise measurement.

9. the length of a steel pipe   **a.** 3 m   **b.** 2.5 m   **c.** 254 cm   _____

10. the mass of a radio   **a.** 4 kg   **b.** 4.4 kg   **c.** $4\frac{1}{2}$ kg   _____

11. the height of a boy   **a.** 5 ft 7 in.   **b.** $5\frac{1}{2}$ ft   **c.** 6 ft   _____

12. the capacity of a water jug   **a.** 1 L   **b.** 0.8 L   **c.** 0.75 L   _____

Mixed Applications

13. Wilma used 22 ounces of catnip to make toys for kittens. She had ordered $1\frac{1}{2}$ pounds of catnip. Which measurement is more precise?

_____

14. About 2,650 yards of roads were repaired in Gladsbury this year. Caryn noted that this is about 1.5 mile. Which measurement is more precise?

_____

15. A toy train was worth $8 in 1910. Its value now is 450% of that amount. How much is the train worth now?

_____

16. An integer and its square differ by 20. If the integer is positive, what is it? If the integer is negative, what is it?

_____

VISUAL THINKING

17. You can form 8 squares with 17 toothpicks, as shown at the right. Draw a picture with 14 squares formed by 24 toothpicks.

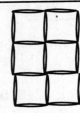

Perimeter of Polygons

Find the perimeter of each polygon.

1.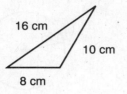

   16 cm
   10 cm
   8 cm

   _____

2.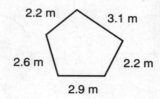

   2.2 m   3.1 m
   2.6 m   2.2 m
         2.9 m

   _____

3.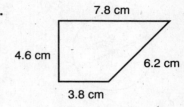

   7.8 cm
   4.6 cm   6.2 cm
         3.8 cm

   _____

Find the perimeter of each square.

4. $s = 45$ ft _____

5. $s = 8.2$ cm _____

6. $s = 17.6$ m _____

Find the perimeter of each rectangle.

7. $l = 5.7$ m, $w = 3.25$ m _____

8. $l = 9\frac{3}{4}$ in., $w = 3\frac{1}{2}$ in. _____

Find the perimeter of each regular polygon.

9. a triangle when $s = 3.6$ in. _____

10. a hexagon when $s = 3\frac{4}{5}$ cm _____

Mixed Applications

11. Find the perimeter of a pendant shaped like a rhombus with a side of length 2.8 cm.

    _____

12. A square and a regular hexagon have the same perimeter. A side of the square is 4.5 in. long. How long is a side of the hexagon?

    _____

LOGICAL REASONING

Find the perimeter of each polygon. Use ⊢——————⊣ to measure. For Exercise 14, an equilateral triangle is built on the middle third of each side in the preceding exercise.

13.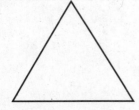

    _____

14.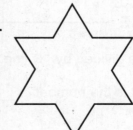

    _____

Circumference of Circles

Find each circumference. Use 3.14 for π.

1.
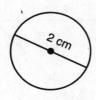
2 cm

_____

2.

7 in.

_____

3.

12 m

_____

4.

15 ft

_____

Find each circumference to the nearest whole number.

5. $d = 9$ m

_____

6. $d = 2.1$ cm

_____

7. $r = 6.1$ cm

_____

8. $r = 7.3$ mm

_____

9. $d = 56$ m

_____

10. $d = 63$ m

_____

11. $r = 2.8$ cm

_____

12. $r = 4\frac{1}{5}$ cm

_____

Find each circumference to the nearest tenth. Use 3.14 for π.

13. $d = 6.4$ mm

_____

14. $r = 0.8$ cm

_____

15. $r = 5.6$ cm

_____

16. $d = 21.1$ cm

_____

Mixed Applications

17. A table top is shaped like a square with half-circles on two ends. One side of the square is 0.8 m. To the nearest meter, what is the perimeter of the table top?

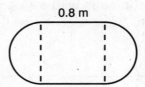
0.8 m

_____

18. A sundial in a park has a circumference of 57 ft. Find the

radius to the nearest foot. _____

NUMBER SENSE

19. When a number is divided by ⁻3, the result is 12 more than

the number. What is the number? _____

Problem-Solving Strategy
Use a Formula

Use a formula to solve each problem.

1. Pilar develops and prints her own photographs. She keeps her darkroom at 68°F. What temperature is this in degrees Celsius?

   _____

2. Kathy dries apples, apricots, and pears for winter storage. She dries them in her oven at 63°C. What Fahrenheit temperature is this?

   _____

Mixed Applications ⟩ **STRATEGIES** • Use a Formula • Guess and Check • Write an Equation • Find a Pattern

Choose a strategy and solve.

3. Tomás tries to keep his greenhouse temperature between 60°F and 70°F at night. Is 23°C too warm, too cold, or an acceptable temperature?

   _____

4. On her patio, Kelly uses a thermometer marked in degrees Celsius. There the temperature is 15°C. What is this in degrees Fahrenheit?

   _____

5. Mark counted 30 passengers on the bus. At each of the next three stops, $\frac{1}{3}$ of the passengers left and 1 passenger got on. After the third stop, how many passengers were on the bus?

   _____

6. The lowest temperature for deep-fat frying at sea level is 350°F, which drops 3°F for each increase of 1,000 ft of altitude. At 4,000 ft above sea level, what would be the lowest temperature in degrees Celsius for deep-fat frying?

   _____

MIXED REVIEW

Find the GCF of each pair of numbers.

1. 18, 30 _____   2. 45, 15 _____   3. 28, 98 _____

Find the LCM of each pair of numbers.

4. 15, 18 _____   5. 14, 35 _____   6. 25, 45 _____

Area
Parallelograms and Triangles

Find the area of each figure.

1.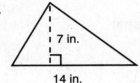

6 cm

18 cm

_____

2. 7 in.

14 in.

_____

3.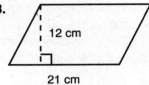

12 cm

21 cm

_____

Find the area of each parallelogram.

4. $b = 7$ cm
$h = 9$ cm

_____

5. $b = 12$ m
$h = 8$ m

_____

6. $b = 21$ in.
$h = 7$ in.

_____

7. $b = 15$ cm
$h = 6$ cm

_____

Find the area of each triangle.

8. $b = 16$ cm
$h = 7$ cm

_____

9. $h = 18$ cm
$b = 6$ cm

_____

10. $b = 22$ in.
$h = 9$ in.

_____

11. $b = 4$ ft
$h = 2\frac{1}{2}$ ft

_____

Mixed Applications

12. Abby plants peonies in a triangular garden with a 12-foot base and an $8\frac{1}{2}$-ft height. If she allows 3 square feet per peony, how many can she plant?

_____

13. A 5-gallon can of asphalt sealant covers about 250 square feet. How many cans of sealant are needed to cover a tennis court that is 78 ft by 27 ft?

_____

NUMBER SENSE

14. A regular hexagon is separated into three congruent rhombuses. Each side of the hexagon is 6 in. long and the height of the hexagon is 10.4 in. What is the area of the hexagon to the nearest square inch?

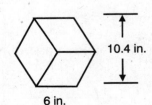

10.4 in.

6 in.

_____

Area of Trapezoids

Find each area.

1.
5 m
4 m
12 m

_____

2.
12 cm
12 cm

_____

3.
10 cm
5 cm
6 cm

_____

4.
20 m
15 m

_____

5.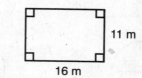
11 m
16 m

_____

6.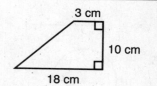
3 cm
10 cm
18 cm

_____

Find the area of each trapezoid.

7. $b_1 = 9$ cm
$b_2 = 11$ cm
$h = 5$ cm

_____

8. $b_1 = 6$ m
$b_2 = 14$ m
$h = 7$ m

_____

9. $b_1 = 24$ cm
$b_2 = 36$ cm
$h = 40$ cm

_____

10. $b_1 = 15$ in.
$b_2 = 6$ in.
$h = 9$ in.

_____

Mixed Applications

11. A plaque is shaped like a trapezoid with a height of 6 in. and bases that measure 3.5 in. and 9.5 in. What is the area of the plaque?

_____

12. A triangle and a rectangle have equal areas and the same height of 8 cm. If the base of the rectangle is 7 cm, how long is the base of the triangle?

_____

VISUAL THINKING

For Exercises 13 and 14, the horizontal or vertical distance between two dots represents 1 unit.

13. Locate point D and connect dots to form trapezoid ABCD with an area of 10 square units.

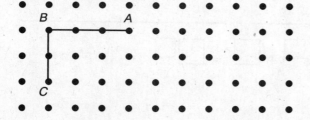

14. Locate point S and connect dots to form trapezoid PQRS with an area of 15 square units.

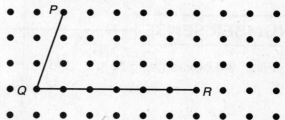

Area of Circles

Find the area of each circle to the nearest whole number. Use 3.14 for π.

1.
10 cm
_____

2.
2.6 cm
_____

3.
4.5 m
_____

4.
20.6 cm
_____

5.
1.5 m
_____

6.
8.2 cm
_____

7.
14.5 m
_____

8.
24.6 m
_____

Find the area of each circle to the nearest tenth.

9. $r = 2$ m _____

10. $r = 9$ m _____

11. $d = 12$ m _____

Find the area of each circle to the nearest hundredth.

12. $r = 0.8$ in. _____

13. $d = 1.4$ ft _____

14. $d = 0.72$ m _____

Mixed Applications

Anzu made a dart board like the one shown at the right. The circle in the middle is the *bull's eye.*

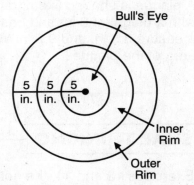

15. What is the area of the bull's eye?

_____

16. What is the area of the outer rim?

_____

17. The outer rim is how many times as large as the bull's eye?

_____

NUMBER SENSE

18. Fill in the boxes using 3, 4, 5, and 7.

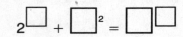

Problem-Solving Strategy
Make a Model

Make a model to solve.

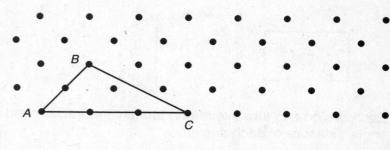

1. Show how you can tesselate a plane using triangles congruent to △ABC. Draw five more triangles.

2. How many degrees has each angle of the octagon?

_____

3. Can you tesselate a plane with octagons like this one?

_____

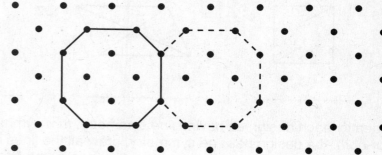

Mixed Applications ▷ **STRATEGIES**
- Guess and Check • Write an Equation
- Make a Model • Use a Formula • Work Backward

Choose a strategy and solve.

4. During three days 567 people attended a fair. On the first day, 172 people came. On the last day 25 more attended than on the second day. How many people came on the last day?

_____

5. Kuri walked $1\frac{1}{2}$ miles at the rate of $4\frac{1}{2}$ miles per hour. She jogged back $1\frac{1}{2}$ miles at 6 miles per hour. How many more minutes did it take her to walk than to jog?

_____

WRITER'S CORNER

6. Look at the octagon figure above. Can you tesselate a plane by combining squares and octagons? Explain.

_____

_____

Symmetry

Draw all the lines of symmetry in each design.

1.
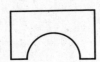

2.

3.

4.

Each design has turn symmetry. Identify the fraction and the angle measure of each design.

5.

6.

7.

8.

_____ _____ _____

Identify each design as having *line* symmetry, *turn* symmetry, or *both*. If a design has line symmetry, draw all the lines of symmetry. If a design has turn symmetry, identify the fraction and the angle measure of each turn.

9.

_____

10.
K
_____

Mixed Applications

11. What type or types of symmetry does every regular polygon have?

12. Dennis bought a tube of oil paint on sale for $2.25. The sale price was what percent of the regular $3.00 price?

_____ _____

VISUAL THINKING

13. Use the line of symmetry to complete the design.

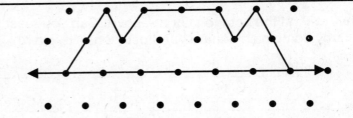

Translations and Reflections

Determine whether each pair of figures represents a *translation* or a *reflection*.

1.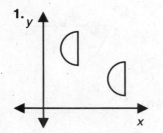

_____

2.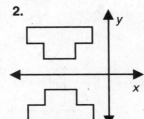

_____

3.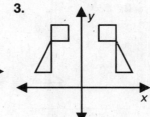

_____

4.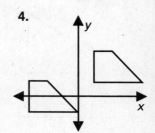

_____

5. Draw the translation image 6 units right and 2 units down.

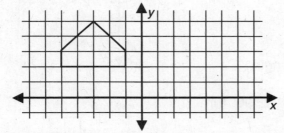

6. Draw the reflection image over the *y*-axis.

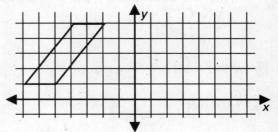

Triangle *ABC* is formed by connecting points (1,2), (3,4), and (6,1).

7. Draw △*ABC* and its reflection over the *y*-axis.

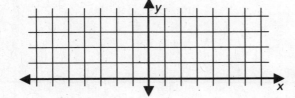

8. Draw △*ABC* and its translation 7 units left and 1 unit down.

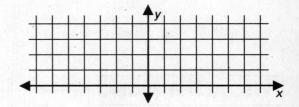

VISUAL THINKING

9. Draw the next line of reflection and the fifth triangle.

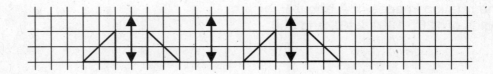

Rotations and Congruent Figures

The flag at the right is rotated in each figure below. The image is unshaded. Write the number of degrees in the turn angle.

1.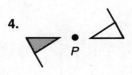

_____

2.

_____

3.

_____

4.

_____

5. On the coordinate grid, plot the points (0,3), (⁻2,1), (⁻4,1) and (⁻6,3). Connect the points in turn and then rotate the figure 180° about the origin. Write the coordinate pairs of the image.

_____

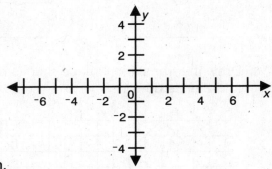

Draw the rotation image of each figure about the origin.

6. 180° turn

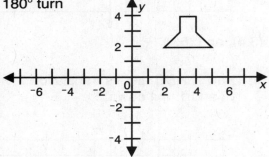

7. 90° turn

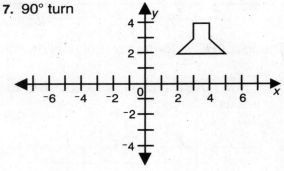

VISUAL THINKING

8. If **A** is rotated to **B** about point *P*, what is the measure of the turn angle?

_____

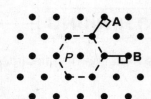

9. Draw the rotation images of **A** about *P* for turn angles of 120°, 180°, 240°, and 300°.

122

Three-Dimensional Figures

Name the figure.

1.

_____

2.

_____

3.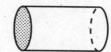

_____

4.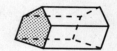

_____

The faces, or surfaces, of some three-dimensional figures are shown.
Name the figure. Is each a polyhedron? Write *yes* or *no*.

5.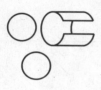

_____

_____

6.

_____

_____

7. □ □ □
   □ □ □

_____

_____

8. △ △
   ▭ ▭
   ▭

_____

_____

Complete the table.

Polyhedron	Number of Faces	Number of Vertices	Number of Edges
9. pentagonal prism			
10. pentagonal pyramid			
11. octagonal prism			
12. octagonal pyramid			

VISUAL THINKING

Imagine a cube formed by folding the pattern shown.

13. Which faces would be opposite each other?
    Write the pairs of numbers on these faces.

_____

```
        3
  6  4  2  5
        1
```

Different Perspectives

Each of the figures in Exercises 1–4 shows one view of a solid figure. Identify the solid as a cylinder, pentagonal prism, pentagonal pyramid, hexagonal prism, hexagonal pyramid, or cube. Give all possible answers.

1.

_____

2.

_____

3.

_____

4.

_____

For each figure, draw the view you would see from the top, the side, and the bottom. For Exercise 6, the top view is already drawn.

5.

6.

Mixed Applications

7. In Drew's science fair project, a ball rolled down a ramp 1 ft in the first second, 4 ft in the second second, and 9 ft in the third second. Following this pattern, how far would it roll in the fourth second?

_____

8. If the ramp in Drew's project were long enough, how far would the ball roll during the first five seconds?

_____

NUMBER SENSE

9. If $\square * \triangle$ means $\frac{\square + \triangle}{3}$, what is the value of $(3 * 5) * (7 * 9)$? _____

124

Surface Area of Pyramids and Prisms

Find the surface area of each figure.

1.

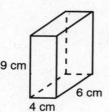

4 cm, 6 cm, 3 cm

_____

2.

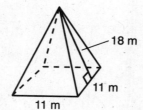

18 m, 11 m, 11 m

_____

3.

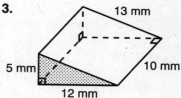

13 mm, 5 mm, 10 mm, 12 mm

_____

4.

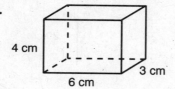

9 cm, 6 cm, 4 cm

_____

5.

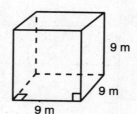

9 m, 9 m, 9 m

_____

6.

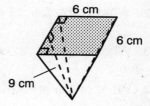

6 cm, 6 cm, 9 cm

_____

Mixed Applications

7. In an experiment with light, Rodney used 6 square polarized filters, 3 in. on a side. What was the total surface area of the filters? Count one face only for each filter.

_____

8. Sandra used a triangular prism 10 cm long to refract light into the spectrum. Each triangular end had an area of 3.5 cm² and sides 3 cm, 3 cm, and 2.6 cm. What was the surface of the prism?

_____

VISUAL THINKING

9. A large cube is painted blue on all sides, and is then cut into 27 congruent cubes. How many of the small cubes are blue

on 3 sides? _____

on 2 sides? _____

on 1 side? _____

on no side? _____

Exploring Surface Area of Cylinders

Chris cut three pieces of contact paper to cover the cylindrical can at the right. Use 3.14 for π.

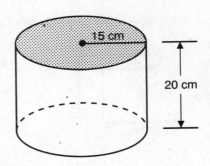

1. What is the area of the circular piece

   for the top? _____

   for the bottom? _____

The curved surface is covered by a rectangular piece of contact paper.

2. What is the height of the rectangle? _____

3. What is the width of the rectangle? _____

4. What is the area of the rectangle? _____

5. What is the total surface area of the cylinder? _____

Find the surface area of each cylinder. Use 3.14 for π.

6.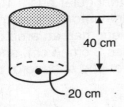

_____

7.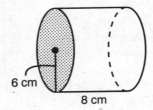

_____

8.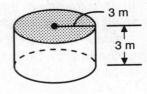

_____

9. Draw the next figure.

Problem-Solving Strategy
Use Estimation

Teresa wants an aquarium for her three tropical fish. The fish are 3.2 cm, 5.4 cm, and 4.5 cm long. Teresa learned that a rectangular tank would be best, with a surface area of 325 cm² for each fish, and 1.5 liters of water for each centimeter of a fish's length.

1. Should the surface area of the tank be about 100 cm², 600 cm², or 1,000 cm²?

   _____

2. The total length of her three fish is about how many centimeters?

   _____

3. About how many liters of water should the tank hold?

   _____

4. Estimate the cost of 3 fish at $4.45 each and $2.53 for fish food.

   _____

Mixed Applications ⟩	STRATEGIES	• Draw a Picture • Write an Equation • Use Estimation • Guess and Check

Choose a strategy and solve.

5. The first day of a sale, the price of a watch was reduced $\frac{1}{3}$. The second day it was reduced $\frac{1}{3}$ again. The third day it was further reduced by $\frac{1}{3}$, selling for $8. What was the original price?

   _____

6. A copper plant tray sold for $16. A month later, the price was increased by 25%. Then the price was lowered by 25% on a sale. What did the plant tray cost then?

   _____

LOGICAL REASONING

7. Out of 30 students, 14 like to skate, 12 like to swim, and 18 like to jog. No student likes all three activities. Six like skating and jogging, and five like jogging and swimming. Four like only swimming. How many students like only skating? To solve, use the Venn diagram at the right.

   _____

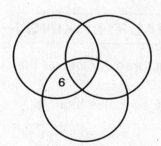

Exploring Volume of Prisms and Cylinders

Find the area of the base and the volume of each prism and cylinder. Use 3.14 for π.

1.
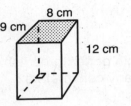
9 cm 8 cm 12 cm

area of base: _____

volume: _____

2.
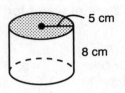
5 cm 8 cm

area of base: _____

volume: _____

3.
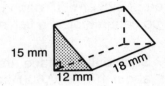
15 mm 12 mm 18 mm

area of base: _____

volume: _____

Find the volume of each figure. Use 3.14 for π.

4.
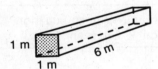
1 m 1 m 6 m

_____

5.
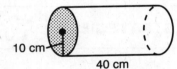
10 cm 40 cm

_____

6.
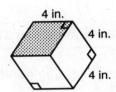
4 in. 4 in. 4 in.

_____

7.
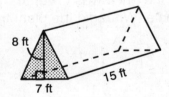
8 ft 7 ft 15 ft

_____

8.
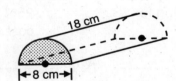
18 cm 8 cm

_____

9.
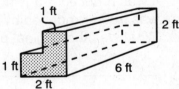
1 ft 2 ft 1 ft 2 ft 6 ft

_____

VISUAL THINKING

Connect three vertices of the cube to form the triangle described.

10. right isosceles triangle

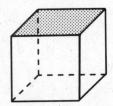

11. equilateral triangle

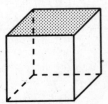

Exploring Volume of Pyramids and Cones

Find the area of the base and the volume of each prism, cylinder, pyramid, or cone. Use 3.14 for π.

1.

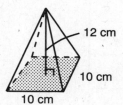

area of base: _____

volume: _____

2.

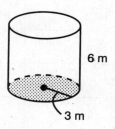

area of base: _____

volume: _____

3.

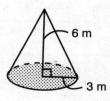

area of base: _____

volume: _____

Find the volume of each figure. Use 3.14 for π.

4.

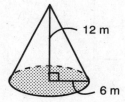

_____

5.

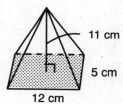

_____

6.

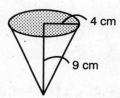

_____

VISUAL THINKING

A triangular pyramid is cut from a corner of a cube 12 in. on an edge. The edges of the pyramid that meet at right angles are 6 in. long.

7. Find the volume of the pyramid. _____

8. Suppose that congruent pyramids are cut from the other seven corners of the cube. What would be the volume of the remaining polyhedron?

_____

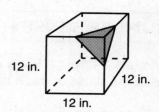

Volume, Capacity, and Mass Relationships

Complete the table for the capacity, volume, and mass of water.

	Capacity	Volume	Mass
1.	3 L		
2.	6 mL		
3.			50 g
4.		300 cm³	
5.	1.5 L		
6.			2.6 kg
7.	.9 kL		
8.		6,000 cm³	

Mixed Applications

9. The total mass of water in two bottles is 1.2 kg. The water in the smaller bottle has 200 g less mass than the water in the larger bottle. What is the volume of water in the larger bottle?

_____

10. The Kelvin temperature scale is 273° higher than the Celsius temperature scale, so 0°C = 273°K. What is the Celsius temperature for 0°K, the Kelvin zero?

_____

NUMBER SENSE

The digits 1 through 9 are arranged so that the sum of the digits in each row is 27.

```
        7
        4
  5 3 9 2 8
        1
        6
```

11. Arrange the nine digits in two intersecting rows so that the sum of the digits in each row is 26.

Exploring Number Patterns

Continue Pascal's triangle.

Pascal's Triangle

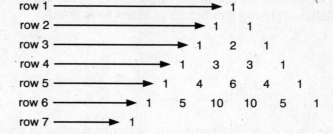

1. Find row 7 of Pascal's triangle.

   _____

2. Find row 8 of Pascal's triangle.

   _____

3. Find row 9 of Pascal's triangle.

   _____

4. What is the triangular number from row 9.

   _____

5. The square number 36 is equal to the sum of what two triangular numbers?

   _____

6. The pentagonal number 22 is equal to the sum of which square and which triangular number?

   _____

   Draw a diagram to support your answer.

LOGICAL REASONING

7. What are the next three numbers in the following pattern: 2, 5, 10, 17, 26, . . . ?

   _____

8. What are the next three numbers in the following pattern: 3, 6, 11, 18, . . . ?

   _____

Geometric Patterns
Tessellations

1. The pictured figure can be used to tessellate a plane. Draw a tessellation using the figure at least four times.

2. Modify a square to create a new figure similar to the one in Exercise 1. Then use your new figure to draw a tessellation.

Mixed Applications

3. Design A in text, page 464, has a regular hexagon surrounded by equilateral triangles that form another larger hexagon. What is the ratio of the area of the triangles to the area of the larger hexagon?

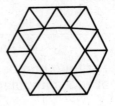

_____

4. For Design A, find the ratio of the area of the smaller hexagon to the area of the larger hexagon.

_____

5. For Design A, find the ratio of the area of the equilateral triangles to the area of the smaller hexagon.

_____

MIXED REVIEW

Find the area of each figure. Use 3.14 for π.

1. a square when $s = 7.3$ in.

_____

2. a parallelogram when $b = 12$ cm, $h = 7$ cm

_____

3. a circle when $r = 3$ in.

_____

4. a triangle when $b = 5.2$ mm, $h = 2.8$ mm

_____

Relations

1. Make a two-column table. List the numbers of Set *A* from least to greatest in the first column. List the numbers of Set *B* from least to greatest in the second column.

 Set *A*   Set *B*

Set *A*: 3 0 5 / 4 1 2

Set *B*: 4 6 2 / 3 5 7

2. If *n* represents any number in Set *A*, what expression represents the number that it is related to in Set *B*?

_____

Use the relation {($^-$2,$^-$6), ($^-$1,$^-$3), (0,0), (1,3), (2,6), (3,9)} for Exercises 3–4.

3. What is the domain of the relation? What is the range of the relation?

_____

_____

4. Make a mapping diagram to show the relation.

Graph points to represent each relation.

5. Domain   Range

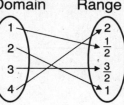

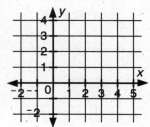

6. {(1, $-\frac{1}{2}$), (2, $^-$1), (3, $-\frac{3}{2}$), (4, $^-$2)}

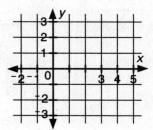

7. Write a word problem to represent the relation shown in the diagram. Make a table to show your results.

_____

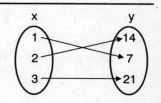

Geometric Relations

1. What happens to the volume of a box if you triple just one dimension?

   _____

2. What happens to the area of a rectangle if you divide both the length and the width by 2?

   _____

3. If you double the base of a triangle, what must you do to keep the area the same?

   _____

4. If you double the width and triple the length of a rectangular box, what must you do to keep the volume the same?

   _____

Mixed Applications

5. A triangle has a height of 5 m. Write an equation showing the relation between the base and the area(A).

   _____

6. The formula for the area of a circle is $A = \pi r^2$. What happens to the area if the radius is tripled?

   _____

7. The formula for the volume of a cylinder is $V = \pi r^2 h$. If you double the radius and triple the height, what happens to the volume?

   _____

8. What is the volume of a box with the dimensions 2 in. by 6 in. by $12\frac{1}{2}$ in.?

   _____

MIXED REVIEW

Find the surface area.

1. a cylinder: $r = 3$ in., $h = 6$ in. _____

2. a rectangular prism: $l = 4$ cm, $w = 2$ cm, $h = 70$ cm _____

Find the volume of each cone (Recall $V = \frac{1}{3}\pi r^2 h$). Use 3.14 for π.
Round to the nearest tenth.

1. radius of base = 3 m, height of cone = 4 m _____

2. radius of base = 4 in., height of cone = 5 in. _____

Exploring Functions

Make a mapping diagram to represent the ordered pairs of each of the relations.

1.

x	y
3	9
2	4
1	1
0	0
⁻1	1
⁻2	4

2.

x	y
⁻8	⁻3
⁻8	3
⁻3	⁻2
⁻3	2
0	⁻1

3. In which diagram does each element of the domain match only one element of the range?

_____

Is each relation a function? Write *yes* or *no*. Explain.

4. {(1,4), (2,4), (3,5)}

_____

_____

_____

5. {(2,3), (5,3), (5,5)}

_____

_____

_____

6.

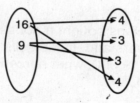

_____

_____

_____

7.

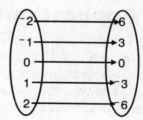

_____

_____

_____

VISUAL THINKING

8. Begin with a square with a side of 1 unit. Make a new square using the diagonal of the first square. Continue this pattern to form 4 squares. Find the area of the fourth square.

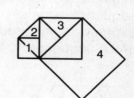

_____

Graphing Functions

Graph the set of ordered pairs. Tell whether the graph represents a function. Write *yes* or *no*.

1. {(⁻1,⁻4), (0,⁻1), (1,2), (2,5)}

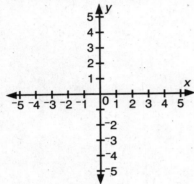

_____

2. {(⁻1,⁻3), (0,⁻1), (1,1), (1,3)}

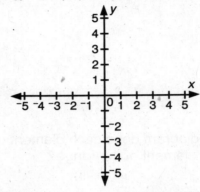

_____

Graph the points that represent the relation. Tell whether the graph represents a function. Write *yes* or *no*.

3. Domain   Range _____

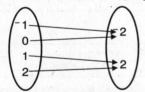

Mixed Applications

4. Two less than three times a number, x, is equal to a number, y. Write an equation. Show three solutions for the equation. Tell whether the equation represents a function. Write *yes* or *no*.

_____

_____

5. Mrs. Hans bought a house for $35,000 ten years ago. If she sells it this year for $119,000, what percent profit will she make?

_____

NUMBER SENSE

6. In the sequence 1, 2, 3, 4, 5, . . . , the value of any term in the sequence equals n, the number of the term itself. Write an expression, in terms of n, that will give the value of any term in the sequence 1, 4, 9, 16, 25.

_____

Exploring The Pythagorean Property

Use a graph-paper diagram with squares to decide whether each triangle is a right triangle.

1. (6, 8, 10)

_____

2. (7, 10, 11)

_____

3. (12, 35, 37)

_____

Use the Pythagorean Property to determine if each triangle is a right triangle.

4. (4, 7, 8) _____

$4^2 +$ _____ $\overset{?}{=}$ _____

_____ $+$ _____ $\overset{?}{=}$ _____

_____ $\Box$ _____

5. (5, 12, 13) _____

_____ $+$ _____ $\overset{?}{=} 13^2$

_____ $+$ _____ $\overset{?}{=}$ _____

_____ $\Box$ _____

6. (5, 6, 9) _____

_____ $+ 6^2 \overset{?}{=}$ _____

_____ $+$ _____ $\overset{?}{=}$ _____

_____ $\Box$ _____

7. (12, 16, 20) _____

$12^2 +$ _____ $\overset{?}{=}$ _____

_____ $+$ _____ $\overset{?}{=}$ _____

_____ $\Box$ _____

8. (9, 12, 15)

_____

9. (4, 5, 6)

_____

10. (10, 24, 26)

_____

NUMBER SENSE

11. The sum of the squares of the numbers 4 and 3 is 25. The ratio of the numbers is 4 : 3. Find two other pairs of numbers whose ratio is $\frac{4}{3}$.

_____

Determine the sum of the squares of those numbers. What is the relation between that sum and 25?

_____

Applying The Pythagorean Property

Find the missing measure. Round to the nearest tenth when necessary.

1.
8 in.
10 in.
?

_____

2.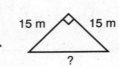
15 m   15 m
?

_____

3.
12 m   ?
5 m

_____

4. a = 6 cm   b = 9 cm

c = _____

5. a = 8 in.   b = 15 in.

c = _____

Tell whether the three sides form a right triangle. Write *yes* or *no*. Support your answer.

6. 15 m, 15 m, 20 m

_____

7. 15 in., 36 in., 39 in.

_____

Mixed Applications

8. Find the length of the guy wire supporting the antenna in the figure.

_____

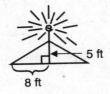
5 ft
8 ft

9. Ted is making a red and yellow quilt with dimensions 72 in. by 90 in. How many sq ft of fabric does he need?

_____

10. Carol caught $1\frac{1}{2}$ times as many fish as Jorge. Together they caught 15 fish. How many did Jorge catch?

_____

EVERYDAY MATH CONNECTION

You want to fence a right triangular piece of land. The lengths of two sides are known: 120 ft and 50 ft. Determine the third side.

_____ How many feet of fencing is required to

enclose the piece of land? _____

Problem Solving
Choose a Strategy

Choose a strategy and solve.

1. Jennifer's age plus her brother's age is 20. The difference between their ages is 4. What are the ages of Jennifer and her brother? (Use Guess and Check or Use a Table).

2. Karia is planning a long run. She leaves her house at 8 a.m. and jogs 4 kilometers per hour. Darlene rides the same route with her bike. She starts at 9 a.m. and travels at 8 kilometers per hour. How far ahead will Darlene be at 11 a.m.?

3. The sum of two numbers is $^-2$. The second number is 13 more than twice the first number. What are the two numbers?

4. The sum of two numbers is $^-4$. Their product is $^-12$. What are the two numbers?

5. The lengths of the sides of a triangle are 9 cm, 40 cm and 41 cm. Do the sides form a right triangle?

6. Leotie buys a car for $9600. She makes a down payment of $1600 and borrows the rest of the money for 3 years. If the loan interest rate is 12% simple interest per year, what is the total amount Leotie will pay for the car?

WRITER'S CORNER

7. Choose a problem-solving strategy and explain how it is helpful for problem solving.

Core Skills: Math, Grade 7, Answer Key

Page 1
1. 1,171
2. 234
3. 23.64
4. 668.61
5. 69.11
6. 62.95
7. 27.5
8. 35.29
9. 442.3
10. 1.3222
11. 731.98
12. 63.036
13. 38.6
14. 262.434
15. Unnex: 7,640 sq mi; Biron: 6,680 sq mi
16. $2, $4, $8, $16
17. 57; The two numbers in each pair have a sum of 10, or 100, or 1,000, and so on.

Page 2
1–2. Check diagram.
1. Pilar, Lori, Mark, Diego, Wendy, Christi
2. 2 blocks
3. 2 min 6 sec
4. 15 combinations

Mixed Review
1–6. Estimates may vary.
1. 60
2. 600,000
3. 400
4. 108,231
5. 337.22
6. 1,499.07

Page 3
1–17. Estimates may vary.
1. 24; 24
2. 350; 420
3. 8; 16
4. 560; 630
5. 90; 130
6. 40; 40
7. 280; 320
8. 70; 80
9. 4
10. 5
11. 4
12. 7
13. 150
14. 4
15. 25
16. 20
17. 4,000
18. $6 to $12
19. about 6 rolls
20. Possible answer: 2.35 x 4.85

Page 4
1. 0.27
2. 0.375
3. 0.08750
4. 540.0
5. 42.200
6. 21.0684
7. 0.162225
8. 0.04872
9. 0.24
10. 0.24
11. 0.049
12. 1.395
13. 72.00
14. 0.0060
15. 7.128
16. 5.22
17. 0.4165
18. 0.06650
19. 0.6474
20. 34.0545
21. 409 mph
22. $224.50
23. 222,222; 333,333; 56

Page 5
1. 227.65
2. 320.
3. 733.5
4. 417,600.
5–20. Estimates may vary.
5. [2] 1.9
6. [15] 13
7. [30] 30
8. [1] 1.2
9. [3] 3.1
10. [7] 7.2
11. [40] 41
12. [12] 12.2
13. [3] 3.3
14. [75] 69
15. [40] 42
16. [100] 90
17. [30] 29.3
18. [150] 154
19. [90] 86.31
20. [30] 32.9
21. 23
22. 23
23. 23
24. 230
25. 230
26. 0.23
27. 1.5
28. 34.5
29. 0.45 – 0.09

Page 6
1–20. Estimates may vary.
1. [15] 15.2
2. [3] 3.19
3. [15] 15

Page 6 (cont.)
4. [600] 606
5. [5] 5.1
6. [50] 52.5
7. [4] 5.06
8. [80] 68
9. [2] 2
10. [8] 8
11. [6] 7
12. [5] 5.4
13. [3] 2.9
14. [7] 6.7
15. [2] 2.16
16. [3] 3.28
17. [10] 9.63
18. [2] 1.967
19. [0.5] 0.485
20. [2] 1.538
21. 3.5; 0.35
22. 146.42; 14.642
23. about 16.5 mm
24. about $2.50
25. 200; 8

Page 7
1. 24 years old
2. Possible answer: 5 pennies, 8 nickels, 2 dimes
3. 4 times
4. 20
5. $4
6. Addie, 4 oz; Blissy, 14 oz; Corky, 8 oz
7. 3: 3; 4: 3 + 1; 5: 9 − 3 − 1; 6: 9 − 3; 7: 9 − 3 + 1; 8: 9 − 1; 9: 9; 10: 9 + 1; 11: 9 + 3 − 1; 12: 9 + 3; 13: 9 + 3 + 1

Page 8
1. 5^2
2. 8^5
3. 9^3
4. 2^4
5. 7^6
6. $(2.3)^2$
7. 625
8. 169
9. 1.44
10. 1
11. 1,000,000
12. 49
13. 1,080 mi
14. 15 gal

Mixed Review
1–4. Estimates may vary.
1. 100
2. 8
3. 120
4. 40
5. 134,288
6. 176
7. 10.35

Page 8 (cont.)
8. 75

Page 9
1. 16; 21; 33
2. about 126 students
3. about 198 students
4. about 18 students
5. about 96 students
6. 2 student tickets
7. 8 ways; For SHOW, 2 choices from each letter on row 2, or 4 in all; then 2 choices from each of those choices, or 8 in all.
8. 16 ways; For DANCE, same as SHOW, then 2 choices from each of the 8, or 16 in all.

Page 10
1. 1983; 1984; 1987
2. about 20,000,000 hours
3. 1975
4. 1965
5. Possible answer: Ticket prices increased.
6. 225

Page 11
1. May
2. September
3. June
4. See page 155.
5. 1989
6. during the warm months
7. 1.18×10^4
8. 2; 5

Page 12
1. Admissions: $0.60; Food: $0.25
2. $252, $105, $63
3. Craft sales: $0.45, School Play: $0.08

Mixed Review
1. 4^3; 64
2. 11^2; 121
3. 5^3; 125
4. $(0.7)^2 \times 4^0$; 0.49

Page 13
1. See page 155.
2. Wednesday
3. Wednesday, Thursday
4. See page 155.
5. Possible answer: The bar graph shows the differences more clearly.
6. 1,000,000

Page 14
1. seventh grade; 20 more students
2. eighth grade; 3 greater

Page 14 (cont.)
3. mean, 21; median, 24; mode, 12
4. mean, 28; median, 32; no mode
5. 8 boxes
6. 11 minutes
7. Ann and Doris

Page 15
1. yes
2. yes
3. no
4. yes
5. yes
6. 2, 4
7. 2
8. 2, 3, 6
9. 2, 3, 4, 6
10. 3
11. 3, 9
12. 2, 3, 9
13. 2, 3, 4
14. 2, 3, 4, 9
15. 2, 3, 4
16. Accept any multiples of 36.
17. Accept any multiples of 30.
18. Accept any multiples of 12.
19. Accept any multiples of 18.
20. Yes; $225 - 75 = 150$, and $150 \div 6 = 25$.
21. No; $225 - 75 = 150$; and $15 \div 4 = 37.5$ or $150 \div 4 = 37$ r2.
22. 5
23. 11

Page 16
1. 1, 2, 3, 6
2. 1, 5, 7, 35
3. 1, 19
4. 1, 3, 13, 39
5. 1, 2, 4, 11, 22, 44
6. 1, 2, 4, 8, 16, 32, 64
7. 1, 2, 4, 7, 8, 14, 28, 56
8. 1, 2, 4, 5, 8, 10, 16, 20, 40, 80
9. composite
10. prime
11. prime
12. composite
13. prime
14. composite
15. prime
16. composite
17. 1 row of 30; 2 rows of 15; 3 rows of 10; 5 rows of 6; 6 rows of 5; 10 rows of 3; 15 rows of 2; 30 rows of 1
18. 2, 3, 4, 6, 8, or 12 people
19. Check problem.

Page 17
1. 9; 2×5; 3×3
2–5. Check drawing.

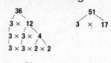

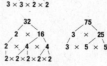

2. $2^2 \times 3^2$
3. 3×17
4. 2^5
5. 3×5^2
6. 300
7. 126
8. 135
9. 250
10. 42, 84, 126, 168
11. 1, 2, 4, 7, 14, 28
12. 169; Each number is the square of a prime number, in order from least to greatest.

Page 18
1. 18: 1, 2, 3, 6, 9, 18; 27: 1, 3, 9, 27; GCF: 9
2. 28: 1, 2, 4, 7, 14, 28; 35: 1, 5, 7, 35; GCF: 7
3. 12: 1, 2, 3, 4, 6, 12; 15: 1, 3, 5, 15; GCF: 3
4. 3×5, 5×7, 5
5. $2 \times 2 \times 2 \times 3$; $2 \times 2 \times 3 \times 3$; 12
6. 3×7; $3 \times 3 \times 5$; 3
7. yes, no, yes
8. 18 groups; 2 maple trees; 3 dogwood trees
9. 5
10. 14
11. 50
12. 16
9–12. Pattern: The numbers are factors of the last number in the set.

Page 19
1–5. Answers will vary.
1. $\frac{6}{8}$
2. $\frac{2}{14}$
3. $\frac{12}{27}$
4. $\frac{4}{5}$
5. $\frac{4}{7}$
6. $\frac{1}{6}$
7. $\frac{1}{9}$
8. $\frac{3}{5}$
9. $\frac{1}{8}$
10. $\frac{3}{4}$

Core Skills: Math, Grade 7, Answer Key (cont.)

Page 19 (cont.)

11. $\frac{1}{8}$
12. $\frac{1}{4}$
13. $\frac{3}{4}$
14. $\frac{5}{9}$
15. $\frac{1}{4}$
16. $\frac{2}{5}$
17. $\frac{2}{7}$
18. $\frac{5}{6}$
19. $\frac{7}{10}$
20. $\frac{1}{3}$
21. $\frac{8}{9}$
22. $\frac{1}{4}$
23. $\frac{1}{2}$
24. $\frac{1}{9}$
25. $\frac{4}{11}$
26. 6 mi
27. 8 hits
28. 4 ways; 2, 3, 6, or 9 groups

Mixed Review

1. 2, 3, 4, 6
2. 2, 3, 5, 6, 10
3. 2, 3, 4, 5, 6, 9, 10
4. 2, 3, 4, 6
5. 10
6. 11
7. 10
8. 10

Page 20

1. $\frac{2}{4}$, $\frac{65}{256}$
2. $1.90
3. Yes; each pair of numbers adds up to 99 and 3 x 99 = 3 x 100 − 3, or 297.
4. 29 customers
5. 3 peanuts
6. 6 squares; 20 triangles

Page 21

1. $\frac{12}{30}$, $\frac{5}{30}$
2. $\frac{10}{15}$, $\frac{12}{15}$
3. $\frac{6}{8}$, $\frac{3}{8}$
4. $\frac{7}{56}$, $\frac{24}{56}$
5. $\frac{5}{6}$, $\frac{3}{6}$
6. $\frac{21}{77}$, $\frac{11}{77}$
7. $\frac{20}{30}$, $\frac{21}{30}$
8. $\frac{5}{20}$, $\frac{16}{20}$
9. $\frac{25}{40}$, $\frac{24}{40}$
10. $\frac{7}{21}$, $\frac{6}{21}$

Page 21 (cont.)

11. $\frac{27}{90}$, $\frac{20}{90}$
12. $\frac{20}{28}$, $\frac{21}{28}$
13. <
14. <
15. >
16. <
17. >
18. <
19. =
20. <
21. >
22. >
23. <
24. =
25. Muskie: 20 lb; Cowboy: 32 lb; Bing: 40 lb
26. Cramer's Market
27. $\frac{2^2}{3^2}$
28. $\frac{2^2}{3^3}$
29. $\frac{6^2}{7^2}$
30. $\frac{9^2}{5^3}$, or $\frac{3^4}{5^3}$
31. $\frac{3^2}{2^5}$

Page 22

1. $\frac{6}{15}$, $\frac{5}{15}$, $\frac{3}{15}$
2. $\frac{5}{30}$, $\frac{18}{30}$, $\frac{20}{30}$
3. $\frac{16}{40}$, $\frac{20}{40}$, $\frac{25}{40}$
4. $\frac{9}{12}$, $\frac{4}{12}$, $\frac{6}{12}$
5. $\frac{6}{30}$, $\frac{15}{30}$, $\frac{20}{30}$
6. $\frac{12}{20}$, $\frac{14}{20}$, $\frac{5}{20}$
7. $\frac{1}{3}$, $\frac{2}{5}$, $\frac{1}{2}$
8. $\frac{7}{12}$, $\frac{2}{3}$, $\frac{5}{6}$
9. $\frac{2}{7}$, $\frac{3}{10}$, $\frac{2}{5}$
10. $\frac{2}{5}$, $\frac{2}{3}$, $\frac{5}{6}$
11. $\frac{3}{10}$, $\frac{4}{9}$, $\frac{1}{2}$
12. $\frac{2}{3}$, $\frac{3}{4}$, $\frac{5}{6}$
13. 24 min
14. 4 cats, 8 dogs
15. 198, 45, 396; Problems will vary.; All of the six answers are divisible by 3 and by 9.

Page 23

1. 9:30 A.M.
2. 6 ft high
3. the ninth day
4. 66 yards

Mixed Review

1. prime; 1, 2
2. prime; 1, 37
3. composite; 1, 3, 9, 27
4. composite; 1, 2, 3, 6, 9, 18, 27, 54

Page 23 (cont.)

5. prime; 1, 19
6. composite; 1, 3, 7, 9, 21, 63

Page 24

1–15. Estimates may vary.

1. 2
2. 5
3. 1
4. 4
5. $7\frac{1}{2}$
6. $7\frac{1}{2}$
7. 6
8. 0
9. 3
10. 8
11. 12
12. 10
13. $1\frac{1}{2}$
14. $13\frac{1}{2}$
15. $4\frac{1}{2}$
16. $\frac{3}{7}$; $\frac{3}{7}$ is less than $\frac{1}{2}$.
17. about 9 lb
18. about 3 mi

19–20. Answers may vary.

19. $\frac{1+3+5}{2+4+6+7+8+9} = $ $\frac{9}{36} = \frac{1}{4}$
20. $\frac{1+2+3+4+5}{6+7+8+9} = $ $\frac{15}{30} = \frac{1}{2}$

Page 25

1–13. Estimates may vary.

1. $[\frac{1}{2}]$ $\frac{4}{9}$
2. $[1]$ $1\frac{1}{8}$
3. $[0]$ $\frac{1}{8}$
4. $[\frac{1}{2}]$ $\frac{1}{2}$
5. $[1]$ $\frac{11}{12}$
6. $[1\frac{1}{2}]$ $1\frac{3}{10}$
7. $[0]$ $\frac{1}{12}$
8. $[2]$ $1\frac{7}{12}$
9. $[\frac{1}{2}]$ $\frac{11}{24}$
10. $[1\frac{1}{2}]$ $1\frac{7}{20}$
11. $[1]$ $1\frac{1}{12}$
12. $[2]$ $1\frac{17}{24}$
13. $[0]$ $\frac{4}{25}$
14. $\frac{1}{3}$
15. 45 videocassettes

16–19. Answers may vary.

16. 1, 2, 1
17. 1, 1, 3
18. 1, 1, 7
19. 3, 1, 1

Page 26
1. 11
2. $8\frac{1}{3}$
3. $19\frac{1}{5}$
4. $9\frac{3}{4}$
5. $12\frac{1}{2}$
6. $25\frac{1}{4}$
7. $7\frac{5}{6}$
8. $25\frac{7}{24}$
9. $10\frac{1}{3}$
10. $12\frac{13}{15}$
11. $22\frac{5}{12}$
12. $21\frac{9}{40}$
13. $7\frac{7}{12}$
14. $10\frac{7}{40}$
15. $14\frac{26}{35}$
16. $14\frac{5}{8}$
17. 19
18. $18\frac{1}{2}$
19. $16\frac{4}{5}$
20. $7\frac{5}{24}$ qt
21. $51\frac{1}{3}$ yd
22. $\frac{1}{6}, \frac{1}{3}, \frac{1}{2}$
23. $\frac{1}{6}, \frac{1}{4}, \frac{1}{3}$

Page 27
1. $6\frac{1}{3}$
2. $11\frac{2}{5}$
3. $2\frac{1}{2}$
4. $8\frac{1}{3}$
5. $7\frac{5}{8}$
6. $7\frac{1}{6}$
7. $13\frac{3}{10}$
8. $8\frac{7}{16}$
9. $4\frac{2}{3}$
10. $3\frac{1}{3}$
11. $1\frac{5}{6}$
12. $8\frac{5}{8}$
13. $6\frac{1}{2}$
14. $\frac{3}{8}$
15. $2\frac{1}{2}$
16. $11\frac{1}{6}$
17. $\frac{3}{4}$
18. $3\frac{7}{10}$
19. $\frac{3}{4}$ hr
20. $1\frac{1}{12}$ hr

Page 27 (cont.)
21.

Page 28
1. 28 games
2. 10 ways
3. 12 games
4. 1 quarter, 2 dimes, 6 nickels
5. Mateo; $\frac{1}{5}$ hr
6. $5\frac{3}{4}$ hr
7. Check problem.

Page 29
1–9. Estimates may vary.
1. 70
2. 44
3. 10
4. 210
5. 355
6. 14
7. 32
8. 51
9. 130
10. 240 stamps
11. no
12. 13
13. $\frac{1}{3}$
14. 8
15. 10 ⬤⬤ ⬤⬤ ⬤⬤ ⬤⬤ ⬤⬤
16. 12 ⬤⬤ ⬤⬤ ⬤⬤ ⬤⬤ ⬤⬤ ⬤⬤
17. 20 ⬤⬤⬤⬤ ⬤⬤⬤⬤ ⬤⬤⬤⬤ ⬤⬤⬤⬤ ⬤⬤⬤⬤

Page 30
1. $\frac{1}{8}$
2. $\frac{2}{5}$
3. $\frac{5}{14}$
4. $\frac{1}{4}$
5. $\frac{7}{16}$
6. $\frac{8}{35}$
7. $\frac{1}{7}$
8. $\frac{1}{2}$
9. $\frac{1}{5}$
10. $\frac{1}{9}$
11. $\frac{3}{4}$
12. $\frac{7}{24}$
13. >
14. <
15. =
16. =
17. <
18. =
19. $\frac{1}{4}$
20. $\frac{1}{5}$

Page 30 (cont.)
21. 8 carnations, 12 zinnias
22. 4, 6
23. 5, 9

Page 31
1. 18
2. 15
3. $5\frac{2}{3}$
4. 39
5. $1\frac{1}{8}$
6. 10
7. 15
8. $8\frac{1}{3}$
9. $2\frac{1}{4}$
10. $12\frac{4}{5}$
11. $6\frac{1}{2}$
12. $1\frac{3}{7}$
13. $7\frac{1}{5}$
14. 21
15. 60
16. 2
17. $2\frac{4}{5}$
18. $\frac{2}{9}$
19. $22\frac{1}{2}$
20. $\frac{1}{12}$
21. $\frac{1}{10}$
22. 15, 18
23. 20, 24
24. 35, 40

Page 32
1. c
2. a
3. b
4. c
5–13. Estimates may vary.
5. 4
6. 15
7. 9
8. 11
9. 4
10. 8
11. 2
12. 30
13. 25
14. about 3 in.
15. 4 people
16. $2 + \frac{1}{3} + \frac{2}{3} = 3$;
Answers may vary.

$$\frac{2 \times 2}{2 \times 2 \times 2} + \frac{2 + 2 + 2}{2 \times 2} = \frac{1}{2} + \frac{3}{2} = 2 \text{ or}$$
$$\frac{2 \times 2}{2 \times 2} + \frac{2}{2 \times 2} + \frac{2}{2 \times 2} = 1 + \frac{1}{2} + \frac{1}{2} = 2$$

Page 33
1. 4
2. 8

Core Skills: Math, Grade 7, Answer Key (cont.)

Page 33 (cont.)
3. 9
4. 3
5. 9
6. 4
7. $7\frac{1}{2}$
8. $3\frac{1}{3}$
9. 6
10. 8
11. 5
12. 6
13. 20
14. 3
15. ▰

Page 34
1. 7
2. $\frac{1}{6}$
3. $\frac{8}{9}$
4. $\frac{3}{10}$
5. $\frac{4}{9}$
6. $\frac{5}{2}$
7. 12
8. 21
9. $2\frac{2}{5}$
10. 3
11. $\frac{1}{2}$
12. 16
13. $1\frac{1}{4}$
14. $\frac{5}{8}$
15. $1\frac{3}{4}$
16. $2\frac{2}{3}$
17. 7
18. $\frac{3}{4}$
19. $\frac{2}{7}$
20. 6
21. $\frac{1}{10}$
22. 5
23. 10
24. 8
25. 17 times
26. 30 books
Mixed Review
1. 6.42×10^3
2. 6.5×10^7
3. 2,000,000
4. 415

Page 35
1. $\frac{1}{15}$
2. $2\frac{2}{3}$

Page 35 (cont.)
3. $8\frac{1}{2}$
4. $\frac{2}{7}$
5. $\frac{2}{3}$
6. $1\frac{1}{2}$
7. 5
8. 9
9. $10\frac{1}{2}$
10. $\frac{3}{4}$
11. $\frac{1}{5}$
12. $7\frac{1}{5}$
13. 6
14. $9\frac{2}{5}$
15. 33
16. 4
17. $8\frac{4}{5}$
18. $4\frac{1}{2}$
19. $2\frac{2}{3}$
20. 14
21. $\frac{3}{8}$
22. $4\frac{1}{2}$
23. $\frac{1}{8}$
24. $2\frac{2}{3}$
25. $1\frac{1}{3}$
26. $13\frac{1}{3}$
27. $3\frac{1}{2}$
28. 12 days
29. 9 oz
30. 2, 3

Page 36
1. $6\frac{3}{4}$ hr
2. 12 games
3. 2 mi
4. 26 fence posts
5. First row: $\frac{5}{2}$; second row: $\frac{1}{4}$, $\frac{1}{2}$; third row: $\frac{1}{20}$, $\frac{1}{10}$; last row: $\frac{1}{50}$, $\frac{1}{25}$
6. Possible answers: Start with $\frac{5}{4}$, multiply by $\frac{2}{5}$; start with $\frac{1}{100}$, multiply by 10.

Page 37
1–18. Answers will vary.
1. =
2. >, ≥, ≠
3. <, ≤, ≠
4. >, ≥, ≠
5. >, ≥, ≠
6. =

Page 37 (cont.)
7. <, ≤, ≠
8. =
9. <, ≤, ≠
10. =
11. <, ≤, ≠
12. >, ≥, ≠; >, ≥, ≠
13. 5 x 6 − 3
14. 5 x 3 − 6 ÷ 3
15. 6 x 3 + 6 x 5
16. $2x + 2$
17. $3x − 5 = 2$
18. $2x + 1 \geq 3$
19. $\frac{1}{100}$
20. $68
Mixed Review
1. 11.733
2. 136.521
3. 0.54

Page 38
1. 25
2. 2
3. 4
4. 7
5. 9
6. 23
7. 306
8. 2.8
9. 10
10. 3 x (8 − 5) = 9
11. (20 + 12) ÷ (4 + 4) = 4
12. (15 − 3) ÷ 12 + 1 = 2
13–14. Sentences may vary.
13. (182 + 157 + 165 + 146 + 178) ÷ 5 = 165.6; mean: 165.6 cm; median: 165 cm
14. (5 x 1.29) + (5 x 1.89) + (3 x 2.79) + (13 x 0.89) = 35.84; $35.84
15. 29

Page 39
1. 7.7
2. 17
3. $1\frac{3}{7}$
4. 9
5. 37
6. 15
7. $t − 19$
8. $34 + (13 + n)$
9–12. Answers will vary.
9. a number, t, decreased by 7
10. the sum of 29 and a number, n
11. 23 decreased by a number, r
12. a number, c, increased by the sum of 5 and 22
13. $n − 5.19$
14. 195
15. A: $d + 5$; B: $d − 2$

Core Skills: Math, Grade 7, Answer Key (cont.)

Page 40
1. Commutative Property of Multiplication
2. Distributive Property
3. Identity Property of Addition
4. Associative Property of Addition
5. 8
6. 4
7. 148
8. 0
9. false; $\frac{1}{5} \neq 5$
10. true; Distributive Property
11. $\frac{2}{5}$
12. Expressions will vary. $7(3 + r)$; $21 + 7r$ dollars
13. Add the preceding two numbers to get the next number.

Page 41
1. $c + 2$
2. $c + 2 = 9$
3. 7 cubes
4. 7 cubes
5. 7
6. Remove 3 cubes from each side.
7. $x = 12$
8. $c = 7$
9. $a = 3$
10. The cubes under the handkerchief plus 3 cubes on the left pan must balance with 8 cubes on the right pan.

Page 42
1. $n = 5$
2. $b = 45$
3. $x = 6\frac{1}{3}$
4. $y = \frac{27}{56}$
5. $y = 55$
6. $c = 1.3$
7. $n + 19 = 221$; $n = 202$
8. $n + 1\frac{2}{3} = 8$; $6\frac{1}{3}$
9. $n + 6\frac{1}{5} = 8\frac{2}{3}$; $n = 2\frac{7}{15}$
10. $n + 5.4 = 23.1$; $n = 17.7$
11. $n + (3 + 2.6) = 9$; 3.4
12. $n + 29 = 113$; $n = 84$
13. $n + 2\frac{2}{3} = 4\frac{1}{2}$; $n = 1\frac{5}{6}$; $1\frac{5}{6}$ miles
14. fewer than
Mixed Review
1. 3
2. 0.4
3. 70

Page 43
1. $a = 72$

Page 43 (cont.)
2. $x = 74$
3. $x = 10\frac{3}{8}$
4. $c = 109$
5. $y = 14$
6. $b = 6\frac{11}{12}$
7. $a = 3\frac{13}{18}$
8. $c = 8.505$
9. $b = 28$
10. $m - 5 = 22$; $m = 27$; 27 students
11. $m + 22.05 = 58.95$; $m = 36.90$; $36.90
12. $p - \frac{1}{6} = \frac{3}{6}$
13. $p = \frac{4}{6}$

Page 44
1. 2.4
2. 11.5
3. 2.002
4. $\frac{49}{72}$
5. 2
6. 100
7. 12
8. $14x$
9. $\frac{n}{9}$
10. a number, z, divided by 11
11. the sum of a number, z, and 11
12. $4\frac{1}{2}$ lb
13. 15 years old
14. 1,320 ft or $\frac{1}{4}$ mile

Page 45
1. $n = 7$
2. $y = 64$
3. $x = 9$
4. $y = 7$
5. $n = 16$
6. $x = 34$
7. $n = 7$
8. $y = 2$
9. $b = 16$
10. $n = 56$
11. $n = 12$
12. $r = 13$
13. $k = 4$
14. $a = 2$
15. $b = 7.5$
16. $n - 19 = 84$; $n = 103$; 103 cards
17. $3n = 12$; $n = 4$; 4 miles per hour
18. $r = \frac{1}{2}$
19. $z = 0$
20. $n = 1$

Page 46
1. 90 seconds or $1\frac{1}{2}$ minutes
2. 8 hours
3. 720 meters
4. 1,300 miles
5. 12 dimes, 3 quarters
6. 375 kilometers
7. 3 blocks
8. $153.45
9. Check problem.

Page 47
1. $x = 36$
2. $a = 35$
3. $n = 87$
4. $n = 30$
5. $x = 120$
6. $b = 135$
7. $n = 119$
8. $x = 24$
9. $y = 165$
10. $e = 180$
11. $a = 100$
12. $b = 112$
13. $\frac{n}{8} = 2.5$; $n = 20$
14. $n + 6.05 = 12.4$; $n = 6.35$
15. $n = \frac{1}{4} \cdot 36 = 9$; 9 years old
16. $\frac{1}{3}n = 24$, $n = 72$; 72 hours
17. about 20
18. about 40
19. about 3

Page 48
1. $4 + c < 11$
2. Remove 4 cubes from each side.
3. $c < 7$
4. Remove 7 cubes from each side.
5. $y < 4$
6. $n > 2$
7. $z < 5$
Mixed Review
1. <
2. >
3. <
4. 11.2
5. 0.25
6. 4.2
7. 0.0082
8. 3.358

Page 49
1. line, segments
2. angle, line
3. ray
4. $\angle K$, $\angle GKJ$, or $\angle JKG$
5. $\overleftrightarrow{ML}$
6. $\overline{UW}$ or $\overline{WU}$

Core Skills: Math, Grade 7, Answer Key (cont.)

Page 49 (cont.)
7. plane
8. angle
9.

Page 50
1. $\vec{RS}$, $\vec{RQ}$
2. $\overline{SR}$, $\overline{SQ}$, $\overline{SP}$
3. $\overleftrightarrow{SR}$ and $\overleftrightarrow{PQ}$, $\overleftrightarrow{SP}$ and $\overleftrightarrow{RQ}$
4. parallel
5. skew
6. intersecting
7. parallel
8. parallel
9. skew
10. Possible answer:

11. Possible answer:

12. Possible answer: 160 lb; 108 lb

Page 51
1–2.

3. parallel, congruent
4. perpendicular, congruent
5. perpendicular
6. neither
7–8. See page 156.
9. $\overline{PY}$
10. parallel
11. 5 bisectors

Page 52
1. 10°; 100°
2. 65°; 155°
3. 22°; 112°
4. 47°; 137°
5. ∠BEF
6. 150°
7. ∠DBC
8. ∠A
9. ∠EFD, ∠BFC, ∠EFB, ∠DFC
10. 120°; 240°
11. 160°
12. 70°, 30°; Accept any
    reasonable drawings.

Page 53
1–3. Accept reasonable
     measurements.
1. 100°
2. 45°
3. 135°
4–6. Check drawings.
4.

5.

6.

7–8. Check constructions.
9. 65°
10. west
11. 21

Page 54
1. convex polygon
2. neither
3. concave polygon
4.

5.

6. true
7. false
8. false
9. true
10. true
11. false
12.

Page 55
1. 10 segments
2. 3 segments, 15 segments,
   36 segments
3. 20 miles
4. $9.50
5. 12 oranges; 6 grapefruit
6. 15 students
7. 15, 21, 55

Page 56
1. obtuse
2. right
3. acute
4. acute
5. right
6. right
7. obtuse
8. right

Page 56 (cont.)
9. acute
10. right
11. obtuse
12. acute
13. isosceles
14. scalene
15. isosceles
16. scalene
17. isosceles
18. equilateral (or isosceles)
19. 100°, 50°
20. 12 posts
21.

Page 57
1. *CK*
2. *RK*
3. *RC*
4. *KCR*
5–7. Check constructions.
5. equilateral
6. isosceles
7. scalene
8. 25°, 65°
9. 14
10. Check drawing. One of three
    possible triangles is shown.

Page 58
1. *BCEF*
2. *ABEF*
3. *ACEF, BDEF, ADEF*
4. rhombus or square
5. trapezoid
6. sometimes
7. always
8. never
9. sometimes
10–12. Drawings may vary.
10.   11.   12.

Page 59
1. 120°
2. 720°
3. 60°
4. 30°
5. 108°
6. 36°
7. 36°
8. 8 miles
Mixed Review
1. $\frac{2}{9}$
2. 35
3. $\frac{4}{5}$
4. 5

Page 60

1. $\frac{1}{5}, \frac{10}{50}$
2. $\frac{1}{2}, \frac{6}{12}$
3. $\frac{2}{5}, \frac{4}{10}$
4. $\frac{3}{4}, \frac{6}{8}$
5. $\frac{1}{3}, \frac{2}{6}$
6. $\frac{5}{6}, \frac{10}{12}$
7. $\frac{3}{5}$, 3 to 5, 3:5; $\frac{5}{3}$, 5 to 3, 5:3
8. $\frac{4}{9}$, 4 to 9; 4:9; $\frac{9}{4}$, 9 to 4, 9:4
9. 20 to 36; 20:36
10. 6:7, $\frac{6}{7}$
11. 3 to 8, $\frac{3}{8}$
12. 8:3, $\frac{8}{3}$
13. 12 to 7, $\frac{12}{7}$
14. 10 to 25; 10:25
15. $\frac{5}{6}$
16. $\frac{4}{9}$
17. $\frac{1}{2}$
18. $\frac{5}{7}$
19. $\frac{5}{9}$
20. $\frac{3}{10}$
21. 6 dogs
22. 30 mph
23. $\frac{15}{60}$

Page 61

1. $\frac{15}{5} = \frac{\blacksquare}{2}$; 6 yd
2. $\frac{42}{6} = \frac{14}{\blacksquare}$; 2 wk
3. $\frac{16}{4} = \frac{\blacksquare}{2}$; 8 eggs
4. $\frac{6}{30} = \frac{8}{\blacksquare}$; 40 min
5. $\frac{50}{2} = \frac{\blacksquare}{3}$; $75
6. $\frac{150}{2} = \frac{\blacksquare}{1}$; 75 km
7. $\frac{230 \text{ mi}}{1 \text{ day}}$
8. $\frac{\$15}{1 \text{ day}}$
9. $\frac{20 \text{ flowers}}{1 \text{ bouquet}}$
10. $\frac{30 \text{ beads}}{1 \text{ necklace}}$
11. $\frac{\$6}{1 \text{ hr}}$
12. $\frac{28 \text{ mi}}{1 \text{ gal}}$
13. $\frac{86 \text{ km}}{1 \text{ hr}}$
14. $\frac{\$0.38}{1 \text{ L}}$
15. $\frac{14.5 \text{ mi}}{1 \text{ hr}}$
16. 11 mi
17. 1 mi
18. One possible answer is: If it takes 72 tokens to play 12 games, how many tokens are needed to play 10 games?

Page 62

1. 4:6, 4 to 6, or $\frac{4}{6}$
2. 2:3, 2 to 3, $\frac{2}{3}$
3. The ratios are equivalent.
4. $\frac{4}{6} = \frac{2}{3}$
5. The cross products are equal.
6. $\frac{6}{8}$
7. $\frac{6}{4}$
8. $\frac{8}{6}$
9. $\frac{4}{6}$
10. $\frac{5}{4}$
11. $\frac{5}{8}$
12. $\frac{24}{6}$

Page 63

1. $x = 4$
2. $c = 81$
3. $k = 2.5$
4. $a = 8$
5. $y = 20$
6. $h = 8$
7. $z = 12$
8. $d = 2$
9. $c = 5$
10. $n = 9$
11. $b = 24$
12. $e = 5$
13. $n = 16$
14. $n = 21$
15. $n = 30$
16. $n = 5$
17. $n = 9$
18. $n = 15$
19. $n = 7.5$
20. $n = 12$
21. $x = 2\frac{2}{3}$
22. $x = 9$
23. $x = 39$
24. 3 rooms
25. 16 boys
26. $\frac{1}{2}$

Page 64

1. 2.1 m
2. 22 in.
3. 241.78 mm
4. 75.36 cm
5. $180
6. $180
7. 22.2 mph
8. 7 mm
9. 20 flowers

Page 65

1. $0.31
2. $0.44

Page 65 (cont.)

3. 6¢
4. $1.11
5. 9¢
6. $0.23
7. $1.25
8. $13.40
9. 32¢
10. $0.21; $0.18; 18-oz box
11. $0.60; $0.66; 5-lb bag
12. 30¢; 26¢; 5 paintbrushes for $1.29
13. $2.00; $1.85; pkg of 8 pairs
14. 3 for $3.29
15. 9.4 in.
16. $0.378/lb; $0.61/lb; $0.198/lb; $0.074/oz

Page 66

1. $x = 14$ cm
2. $x = 4.5$ in.
3. $x = 6$ mm
4. $x = 15$ cm
5. $x = 15$ mm
6. $x = 2$ m
7. $x = 6$ cm
8. $x = 9$ in.
9. yes
10. $2.20/lb

Mixed Review

1. about 3
2. about 1
3. about 32
4. about 5

Page 67

1. $x = 4$ cm
2. $x = 3.2$ m
3. $x = 18$ mm
4. $x = 20$ in.
5. $x = 6$ cm
6. $x = 14$ in.
7. $h = 24$ ft
8. 5 dimes, 3 quarters or 10 dimes, 1 quarter
9. 2.5 cm, 4.5 cm, 5.5 cm
10. 10 cm, 18 cm, 22 cm

Page 68

1. $\frac{20}{100}$, 0.20, 20%
2. $\frac{78}{100}$, 0.78, 78%
3. 29%
4. 2%
5. 75%
6. 95%
7. 37%
8. 11%
9. $\frac{54}{100}$, 0.54
10. $1.82
11. 26%; 64%

Page 69
1. 0.85
2. 0.03
3. 0.95
4. 0.17
5. 0.68
6. 0.162
7. 0.04
8. 1.55
9. 0.50
10. 0.715
11. 0.888
12. 1.03
13. 6%
14. 78%
15. 143%
16. 60.7%
17. 52%
18. 11%
19. 109%
20. 140.6%
21. 165%
22. 10.12; 1,012%
23. 37.8; 3,780%
24. 0.82
25. 351 mi
26. $\frac{28}{15} \div \frac{7}{5}; \frac{7}{5} \div \frac{28}{15}$

Page 70
1. $\frac{71}{100}$
2. $\frac{3}{100}$
3. $\frac{41}{10}$, or $4\frac{1}{10}$
4. $\frac{8}{5}$, or $1\frac{3}{5}$
5. $\frac{14}{25}$
6. $\frac{33}{50}$
7. $\frac{39}{50}$
8. $\frac{21}{25}$
9. $\frac{7}{25}$
10. 11%
11. 75%
12. 63%
13. 70%
14. 192%
15. 97%
16. 70%
17. $62\frac{1}{2}$%
18. 88%
19. 80%
20. $\frac{9}{50}$
21. $\frac{21}{100}$
22. 3%
Mixed Review
1. 3
2. 2
3. 7

Page 70 (cont.)
4. $\frac{1}{12}$

Page 71
1. 60%
2. 350%
3. 1.5%
4. 480%
5. 250%
6. 228%
7. 0.7%
8. 150%
9. 0.6%
10. 0.09
11. 0.55
12. 0.025
13. 2.2503
14. 4.106
15. 0.0002
16. 1.6
17. 0.069
18. 1.205
19. $\frac{1}{800}$
20. $\frac{3}{500}$
21. $\frac{7}{400}$
22. $\frac{6}{5}$
23. $\frac{7}{4}$
24. $\frac{1}{40}$
25. 2
26. $\frac{1}{1,250}$
27. $\frac{3}{5,000}$
28. 6.5%
29. $350,000
30. Answers may vary.
   2 quarters and a dime

Page 72
1. 1.2
2. 127.5
3. 15
4. 72
5. 67.2
6. 37.8
7. 13.5
8. 103.6
9. 1.26
10. 9.8
11. 32.4
12. 180
13. $70
14. 33.8
15. 0.323
16. $34.50
17. about 28.26 in.
18. $472.80
19. $517.13

Page 73
1. $1,920
2. $1,440
3. $6,000
4. $5,280
5. $1,680
6. $4,800
7. $2,880
8. $8,960
9. 8%
10. $4\frac{2}{3}$ mi/hr
11. 42 and 26
12. 9.87 − 6.54 + 3.21 = 654%

Page 74
1. 108°
2. 90°
3. 72°
4. 54°
5. 36°
6. See page 156.
7. meals: 30%, $270; lodging: 25%, $225; transportation: 20%, $180; recreation: 15%, $135; other: 10%, $90
8. See page 156.
Mixed Review
1. 6.287
2. 3.375
3. 1

Page 75
1. $2.10
2. $33.15
3. $29.70
4. $19.50
5. $23.55
6. $72.00
7. $0.48
8. $6.75
9. $5.52
10. $3.90
11. $4.82
12. $14.10
13. $68
14. $20.82
15. $250.75
16. $44.84
17. $15.30
18. $425
19. $12.84
20. $9.58
21. $16.59
22. $40.80
23. $30.10
24. Check problem.

Page 76
1. $\frac{40}{100} = \frac{n}{10}$
2. $n\% \times 10 = 7$

Core Skills: Math, Grade 7, Answer Key (cont.)

Page 76 (cont.)
3. $0.40 \times n = 4$
4. b
5. a
6. c
7. 90%

Page 77
1. 40%
2. 25%
3. 34%
4. 30%
5. 68%
6. 72%
7. 20%
8. 50%
9. $55\frac{5}{9}\% \approx 55.6\%$
10. 60%
11. 25%
12. 20%
13. $133\frac{1}{3}\%$
14. $15.74

Mixed Review
1. $x = 1.9$
2. $z = 12$
3. $c = 2.53$
4. $b = 0.265$

Page 78
1. 40
2. 500
3. 40
4. 200
5. 56
6. 600
7. 12
8. 100
9. 500
10. 1,600
11. $12,000
12. 85¢
13. $1.55, $13.95
14. $16.00, $16.00

Page 79
1–3. Estimates may vary.
1. c
2. c
3. a
4–12. Estimates may vary.
4. 50%
5. $33\frac{1}{3}\%$
6. 25%
7. 12%
8. $33\frac{1}{3}\%$
9. 25%
10. 50%
11. 50%

Page 79 (cont.)
12. 50%
13. 200
14. 80
15. 70%
16. 15%
17. 77
18. $28

Page 80
1. 98
2. 1
3. ⁻1,011
4. 15
5. (number line)
6. ⁻14
7. ⁻15
8. 27
9. 3.5
10. 78
11. 21
12. 4.2
13. 15
14. 101
15. never
16. always
17. 14°C
18. $24.50
19. ⁻10, ⁻6, 2
20. ⁻1, 0, 4
21. ⁻8, ⁻3, 6

Page 81
1. 2
2. ⁻4
3. 0
4. ⁻3
5. ⁻1
6. ⁻1
7. 11
8. ⁻20
9. 0
10. ⁻25
11. 54
12. ⁻3
13. 22
14. 10
15. 3
16. ⁻6
17. ⁻10
18. 1
19. 35
20. ⁻10
21. ⁻6
22. 22
23. ⁻9
24. ⁻10°C
25. $\frac{7}{12}$ yd
26. $a = b = 0$ or $a = ⁻b$

Page 82
1. (R)(R)(R)
   (B)(B)
   4, 4, 2, 2
2. (R)(R)
   (B)(B)(B)(B)
   2, 2
3. 2, 2; ⁻2 − (⁻4) = ⁻2 + 4
4–6. Models may vary.
4. (R)(R)(R)(R)(R)(R)(R)(R)(R)
   (B)(B)(B)(B)(B)(B)
   4
5. (R)(R)(R)(R)(R)(R)(R)(R)
   (B)(B)(B)(B)(B)(B)
   ⁻10
6. (R)(R)(R)(R)(R)
   (B)(B)(B)(B)(B)(B)(B)(B)
   10
7. $6 + (⁻8) = ⁻2$
8. $(⁻8) + 6 = ⁻2$
9. $8 + 6 = 14$
10. (B)(B)(B)(B)(B)(B)(B)(B)
    (R)(R)(R)(R)(R)(R)
    ⁻4

Page 83
1. 4
2. 6
3. ⁻5
4. 15
5. 19
6. 14
7. ⁻7
8. 24
9. 6
10. 4
11. ⁻4
12. ⁻6
13. 5
14. ⁻5
15. ⁻1
16. ⁻6
17. ⁻8
18. 2
19. ⁻13
20. 0
21. 0
22. 19°C or ⁻19°C
23. $3.49
24. ⁻101
25. 119
26. ⁻582
27. 65

Page 84
1. ⁻3 + (⁻3) = ⁻9; ⁻9. ⁻6 (number line)
2. ⁻10, ⁻15, ⁻20, ⁻25
3. ⁻27, ⁻18, ⁻9, 0
4. 6, 9, 12, 15, 18
5. 24
6. ⁻24
7. ⁻24
8. 28
9. ⁻28

Core Skills: Math, Grade 7, Answer Key (cont.)

Page 84 (cont.)
10. -28
11. -27
12. -3
13. 1
14. -4, 16
15. -5, -5, -5, -125
16. -52, -48, -44
17. Add 4 to each term, or notice that -64 = -16 x 4, -60 = -15 x 4, -56 = -14 x 4 and so on.

Page 85
1. 7
2. -6
3. -9
4. -9
5. 9
6. -11
7. 9
8. 0
9. -5
10. -7
11. 4
12. 1
13. -4
14. 8
15. 9
16. 2
17. -5
18. 36
19. -5
20. -2
21. 4
22. -2.5°C
23. $56.25
24. 20 pounds
25. 20%
Mixed Review
1. 82°; 172°
2. 54°; 144°
3. 1°; 91°
4. 49°; 139°
5. 25°; 115°
6. 17°; 107°

Page 86
1. Distributive Property of Multiplication over Addition
2. Commutative and Associative Properties of Addition
3. Associative Property of Multiplication
4. -6
5. -16
6. 0
7. 1
8. -1
9. 8
10. -13

Page 86 (cont.)
11. -23
12. 2
13. -6
14. -3 · 4; -3 · -5; -12 + 15 = 3
15. 12 years old
16. $33
17. 3 and -8

Page 87
1. $x - 7$
2. $6c$
3. $n + 12$
4. $z \div 13$, or $\frac{z}{13}$
5. -2
6. 3
7. 3
8. -4
9. -9
10. 1
11. 11
12. 0
13. -5
14. $6,125
15. Let x = the number of adults. Number of students: $3x + 4$
Mixed Review
1. acute
2. right
3. obtuse
4. scalene
5. equilateral
6. isosceles

Page 88
1. add -5
2. subtract 5
3. divide by 3
4. divide by -8
5. multiply by 3
6. subtract -6
7. $n = 6$
8. $x = 3$
9. $y = -12$
10. $t = 14$
11. $y = -3$
12. $a = 9$
13. $c = -8$
14. $y = 3$
15. $r = -7$
16. $x = -3$
17. $z = -7$
18. $t = 3$
19. 222 people
20. 9
21. 4th floor

Page 89
1. (2, 6)
2. (-2, 1)
3. (-7, -5)

Page 89 (cont.)
4. (7, -2)
5. G
6. E
7. I
8. H
9. See page 156.
10. quadrilateral
11. (-7, -3), (-2, -2), (0, -5), (-5, -9)
12. -14 + 5 = -9; $9
13. Check problem.

Page 90
1. y-coordinates: 4, 5, 6
2. y is 3 more than x
3. Add 3 to the value of x to find y.
4. $y = x + 3$
5–6. See page 156.
7. The value of y is three times the value of x.
8. $y = 3x$
9. See page 156.
10. $y = 1$

Page 91
1–12. Answers will vary.
1. $\frac{-5}{1}$; $\frac{5}{-1}$
2. $10\frac{1}{5}$; 1,020%
3. $5\frac{2}{5}$%; 0.054
4. $\frac{6}{7}$; 85.7%
5. 6.3%; $\frac{63}{1,000}$
6. 7%; 0.07
7. 1.1%; 0.011
8. $\frac{3}{10}$; 30%
9. $2\frac{1}{2}$
10. 5%
11. $2.25
12. $1.17
Mixed Review
1. $\frac{(2 \text{ mi})}{(1/2 \text{ hr})} = \frac{4 \text{ mi}}{1 \text{ hr}}$
2. $\frac{22 \text{ km}}{2 \text{ hr}} = \frac{11 \text{ km}}{1 \text{ hr}}$
3. $\frac{(4 \text{ cm})}{(1/4 \text{ min})} = \frac{16 \text{ cm}}{\text{min}}$
4. $n = 9$
5. $x = 17.5$
6. $y = 36$

Page 92
1. 0.15
2. 0.98
3. 2.25
4. 0.65
5. 2.6
6. 0.042
7. 0.62
8. 0.24
9. $\frac{8}{25}$

Core Skills: Math, Grade 7, Answer Key (cont.)

Page 92 (cont.)

10. $\frac{3}{4}$

11. $3\frac{3}{5}$

12. $\frac{89}{100}$

13. $\frac{127}{200}$

14. $\frac{11}{50}$

15. $\frac{7}{20}$

16. $2\frac{3}{10}$

17. piano

18. $\frac{3}{8}$

19. $\frac{63}{100}$

20. 10.38 cm long x 8.25 cm wide

21. 6.25%

22. 31.25%

23. 43.75%

Page 93

1. 0.1111111 . . ., $0.\overline{1}$

2. $0.\overline{2}$

3. $0.\overline{5}$

4. $1.\overline{1}$

5. $0.0\overline{2}$

6. $0.\overline{263}$

7. $0.381\overline{244}$

8. $0.\overline{113}$

9. $3.129\overline{831}$

10. $0.41\overline{6}$

11. $1.\overline{6}$

12. $2.\overline{6}$

13. $2.\overline{4}$

14. $1.\overline{1}$

15. $0.58\overline{3}$

16. $0.\overline{36}$

17. $0.3\overline{8}$

18. $3.\overline{3}$

19. $1.\overline{2}$

20. $0.0\overline{1}$

21. $\frac{10}{27} = 0.\overline{370}$; $\frac{20}{27} = 0.\overline{740}$; $\frac{80}{27} = 2.\overline{962}$

Page 94

1. terminating; 0.2125

2. terminating; 0.78125

3. repeating; $0.3958\overline{3}$

4–9. Answers may vary.

4. $\frac{-11}{5}$

5. $\frac{-5}{1}$

6. $\frac{2}{1}$

7. $\frac{41}{8}$

8. $\frac{11}{50}$

9. $\frac{7}{9}$

10. terminating; 0.3125

11. terminating; 0.036

12. terminating; 0.12

13. repeating; $0.\overline{54}$

Page 94 (cont.)

14. repeating; $0.2\overline{7}$

15. repeating; $0.4\overline{6}$

16. repeating; $1.\overline{2}$

17. repeating; $0.\overline{18}$

18. terminating; 0.6

19. a. $\frac{-3}{4}$; -0.75; b. $\frac{-1}{10}$; -0.1; c. $\frac{1}{4}$; 0.25; d. $\frac{19}{20}$; 0.95

Page 95

1. $\frac{25}{2}$

2. $\frac{-69}{8}$

3. $\frac{-13}{1}$

4. $\frac{13}{100}$

5. $\frac{857}{100}$

6. $\frac{-1,063}{100}$

7. $\frac{26}{1}$

8. $\frac{-4}{5}$

9. >

10. >

11. <

12. >

13. <

14. >

15. =

16. >

17. <

18. -7, -5.8, $1\frac{2}{3}$, $3\frac{5}{8}$

19. -0.5, $\frac{-5}{12}$, $\frac{-7}{32}$, $\frac{7}{9}$, 1.1

20. Connie's was the greater by 0.0125 in.

21. $40.00

22. 7

Page 96

1–15. Answers will vary.

1. -5.5

2. 0.31

3. $\frac{1}{2}$

4. 1.635

5. 0.65

6. -15.25

7. $\frac{29}{64}$

8. 2.51

9. $\frac{5}{6}$

10. 1.945

11. $1\frac{1}{4}$

12. -0.19

13. 400.705

14. 4.075

15. 1.19

16. 80.4 mph

17. 8.1925 mm

18. Check riddle.

Page 97

1. 1,000,000; 10,000,000

2. 0.0001; 0.00001

3. 3 x 3, 9; 3, 3; 1, 1

4. $\frac{1}{3^2}$, $\frac{1}{9}$; $\frac{1}{3^3}$, $\frac{1}{27}$; $\frac{1}{3^4}$, $\frac{1}{81}$

5. 10^{-5}

6. 3^{-9}

7. 10^{-11}

8. 6^{-3}

9. $\frac{1}{10^9}$

10. $\frac{1}{2^{14}}$

11. $\frac{1}{4^8}$

12. $\frac{1}{10^{12}}$

13. 10^{-5}

14. 10^{-7}

Mixed Review

1. $x = 6$ cm

2. $x = 5$ mm

3. $0.32

4. $0.56

5. $2.19

Page 98

1. 10^{-5}

2. 10^{-4}

3. 7.05

4. 2.119

5. 3.64×10^{-5}

6. 7.51×10^{-3}

7. 1.0005×10^{-1}

8. 1.094×10^{3}

9. 9.9×10^{-7}

10. 4.101×10^{-2}

11. 1.05×10^{4}

12. 8.9×10^{3}

13. 0.00074

14. 0.083

15. 0.00195

16. 0.000028

17. 5,450

18. 920,000

19. 0.0006091

20. 0.909

21. 300,000 km/sec

22. 6.048×10^{5} sec

23. 3.62×10^{-6}, 3.62×10^{-2}, 4.1×10^{-2}, 4.1×10^{7}, 4.1×10^{9}

Page 99

1. 225

2. 8

3. 100

4. -5

5. $\frac{1}{16}$

6. 14

7. 4.4521

8. $\frac{-1}{11}$

9. $\frac{4}{81}$

Core Skills: Math, Grade 7, Answer Key (cont.)

Page 99 (cont.)
10. 0.8
11. 64
12. 0.06
13. 4.9
14. 8.5
15. 12.1
16. 2.2
17. 10.0
18. 7.8
19. 17.3
20. 22.0
21. 4.6
22. 7.5
23. 3.6
24. 9.5
25. 10.5
26. 9.3
27. 15.8
28. 4.1
29. 400 ft
30. 11.2 cm
31. $252
32. 20.2 m
33. b

Page 100
1. rational
2. irrational
3. rational
4. rational
5. rational
6. irrational
7. rational
8. irrational
9. real, rational, integer
10. real, rational
11. real, irrational
12. real, rational
13. real, irrational
14. No; She bought only $6\frac{1}{12}$ yd; she is short by $\frac{7}{12}$ yd.
15. Yes; The square will be 14 ft x 14 ft.
16. 2.45 sec

Page 101
1. 1,300 people
2. $11
3. $2.36
4. 12 hr
5. 7 adults, 13 students
6. 3 or 0

Page 102
1. (H, T), (H, R), (H, S), (H, L), (H, P)

Page 102 (cont.)
2. (T, H), (T, R), (T, S), (T, L), (T, P); (R, H), (R, T), (R, S), (R, L), (R, P); (S, H), (S, T), (S, R), (S, L), (S, P); (L, H), (L, T), (L, R), (L, S), (L, P); (P, H), (P, T), (P, R), (P, S), (P, L)
3. 15 pairs
4. 5 + 4 + 3 + 2 + 1 = 15
5. 28 combinations
6. 10 triangles

Page 103
    120 ways
1. 5 choices
2. 4 seats
3. 3 seats
4. 2 seats
5. 1 seat
6. 120 arrangements; yes; For each seat filled, the number of ways of filling the next seat is one less.
7. 5,040 ways
8. 720 orders
9. 6,720 results
10. 120
11. 720
12. 5,040
13. 362,880

Page 104
1. yes
2. no
3. no
4. no
5. neither
6. certain
7. 3:4 or $\frac{3}{4}$
8. 38.5%
9. 2:4 or $\frac{1}{2}$
10. The side opposite 6 must be at least one. 6 + 1 ≠ 6.

Page 105
1. $\frac{1}{8}$
2. $\frac{1}{8}$
3. $\frac{1}{2}$
4. $\frac{1}{4}$
5. $\frac{3}{4}$
6. $\frac{7}{8}$
7. $\frac{1}{2}$
8. $\frac{3}{8}$
9. $\frac{1}{8}$

Page 105 (cont.)
10. $\frac{2}{5}$
11. $\frac{1}{5}$
12. Answers may vary.

Page 106
1. $\frac{1}{5}$
2. $\frac{4}{5}$
3. $\frac{9}{25}$
4. $\frac{4}{25}$
5. $12
6. 56 ways
7. Answers may vary.

Page 107
1. $\frac{3}{10}$
2. red, blue, or green
3. $\frac{2}{5}$
4. yes; It is only $\frac{1}{10}$ less than $\frac{2}{5}$.
5. yes; 22 out of 50 is close to 20 out of 50.
6. 200 times; 100 times
7. 5 times
8. 25 times
9. 12 times
10. 20 times
11. 36 hits

Page 108
1. $\frac{1}{24}$
2. $\frac{1}{24}$
3. $\frac{5}{24}$
4. $\frac{1}{8}$
5. 0
6. 0
7. $\frac{1}{36}$
8. $\frac{1}{12}$
9. $\frac{1}{12}$
10. $\frac{1}{4}$
11. $\frac{5}{36}$
12. $\frac{1}{72}$
13. $\frac{5}{108}$
14. $\frac{1}{9}$

Mixed Review
1. $\frac{3}{4}$ x 96 = 72
2. $\frac{21}{50}$ x 100 = 42
3. $\frac{9}{100}$ x 40 = 3.6
4. 0.05 x 36 = 1.8
5. 0.12 x 500 = 60
6. 0.035 x 500 = 17.5

152

Core Skills: Math, Grade 7, Answer Key (cont.)

Page 109

1. $\frac{4}{12} \times \frac{3}{11} = \frac{1}{11}$
2. $\frac{3}{12} \times \frac{3}{11} = \frac{3}{44}$
3. $\frac{2}{12} \times \frac{4}{11} = \frac{2}{33}$
4. $\frac{4}{12} \times \frac{3}{11} = \frac{1}{11}$
5. $\frac{3}{12} \times \frac{2}{11} = \frac{1}{22}$
6. $\frac{1}{22}$
7. $\frac{2}{12} \times \frac{1}{11} = \frac{1}{66}$
8. $\frac{3}{12} \times \frac{4}{11} = \frac{1}{11}$
9. $\frac{2}{12} \times 0 = 0$
10. $\frac{3}{12} \times \frac{3}{11} = \frac{3}{44}$
11. $\frac{2}{21}$
12. $\frac{2}{21}$
13. $\frac{8}{105}$
14. $\frac{5}{17}$
15. 15 ways: $\frac{1}{1}, \frac{1}{2}, \frac{1}{4}, \frac{1}{6}, \frac{1}{8}, \frac{2}{1}, \frac{2}{6}, \frac{4}{1}, \frac{4}{6}, \frac{6}{1}, \frac{6}{2}, \frac{6}{4}, \frac{8}{1}, \frac{8}{6}, \frac{6}{8}$

Page 110

A possible number might be
   5 beans.
1. A possible ratio might be 5:55.
2. $\frac{5}{55} = \frac{51}{x}$; $x = 561$
3. total number of birds at large in the population
4. Assign each spinner item a digit. The probability of any item occurring is the number of times its digit occurs in the sample of random numbers, divided by 20. This ratio, multiplied by 100, will simulate the number of times the spinner item would be selected randomly in 100 spins.

Mixed Review

1. 40%
2. 24
3. 6
4. 50%
5. 1,200
6. 42

Page 111

1. The run can be used as a simulation to determine what percentage of stamping errors occurred during the 3-hour run.
2. about 900 cans
3. about 3,000 cans
4. about 600 cans
5. 256 ways
6. about 2,400 cans
7. 0.00586

Page 112

1. 30 oz
2. 85 min
3. 3.10 kg
4. 53 mm
5. 50 hr
6. 6.1 in.
7. 50 ft
8. 9.0 ft
9. c
10. b
11. a
12. c
13. 22 ounces
14. 2,650 yards
15. $36
16. 5, -4
17.

Page 113

1. 34 cm
2. 13.0 m
3. 22.4 cm
4. 180 ft
5. 32.8 cm
6. 70.4 m
7. 17.9 m
8. $26\frac{1}{2}$ in.
9. 10.8 in.
10. $22\frac{4}{5}$ cm
11. 11.2 cm
12. 3 in.
13. 3 units
14. 4 units

Page 114

1. 6.28 cm
2. 43.96 in.
3. 37.68 m
4. 94.2 ft
5. 28 m
6. 7 cm
7. 38 cm
8. 46 mm
9. 176 m
10. 198 m
11. 18 cm
12. 26 cm
13. 20.1 mm
14. 5.0 cm
15. 35.2 cm
16. 66.3 m
17. 4 m
18. 9 ft
19. -9

Page 115

1. 20°C

Page 115 (cont.)

2. 145.4°F
3. too warm
4. 59°F
5. 11 passengers
6. 170°C

Mixed Review

1. 6
2. 15
3. 14
4. 90
5. 70
6. 225

Page 116

1. 108 cm²
2. 49 in.²
3. 252 cm²
4. 63 cm²
5. 96 m²
6. 147 in.²
7. 90 cm²
8. 56 cm²
9. 54 cm²
10. 99 in.²
11. 5 ft²
12. 17 peonies
13. 9 cans
14. 94 in.²

Page 117

1. 34 m²
2. 144 cm²
3. 40 cm²
4. 150 m²
5. 176 m²
6. 105 cm²
7. 50 cm²
8. 70 m²
9. 1,200 cm²
10. 94.5 in.²
11. 39 in.²
12. 14 cm
13.
14.

Page 118

1. 314 cm²
2. 5 cm²
3. 64 m²
4. 333 cm²
5. 7 m²
6. 53 cm²
7. 660 m²
8. 475 m²
9. 12.6 m²
10. 254.3 m²

Core Skills: Math, Grade 7, Answer Key (cont.)

Page 118 (cont.)
11. 113.0 m²
12. 2.01 in.²
13. 1.54 ft²
14. 0.41 m²
15. 78.5 in.²
16. 392.5 in.²
17. 5
18. 5, 7, 3, 4

Page 119
1.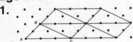
2. 135°
3. no
4. 210 people
5. 5 minutes
6. Yes. The space between any four connecting octagons occupying two rows can be filled by a square.

Page 120
1–4.
5. $\frac{1}{2}$, 180°
6. $\frac{1}{2}$, 180°
7. $\frac{1}{6}$, 60°
8. $\frac{1}{3}$, 120°
9. both; $\frac{1}{3}$, 120°
10. line
11. line symmetry and turn symmetry
12. 75%
13.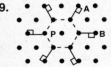

Page 121
1. translation   3. reflection
2. reflection   4. translation
5–9. See page 156.

Page 122
1. 90°
2. 180°
3. 270°, or 90° counterclockwise
4. 180°
5. (0, ⁻3), (2, ⁻1), (4, ⁻1), (6, ⁻3). See page 156 for grid.
6–7. See page 156.
8. 60°
9.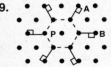

Page 123
1. pentagonal pyramid
2. triangular pyramid
3. cylinder
4. pentagonal prism
5. cylinder, no
6. triangular pyramid, yes
7. cube, or rectangular prism, yes
8. triangular prism, yes
9. 7, 10, 15
10. 6, 6, 10
11. 10, 16, 24
12. 9, 9, 16
13. 6, 2; 4, 5; 1, 3

Page 124
1. hexagonal or pentagonal prism
2. pentagonal prism or pyramid
3. pentagonal pyramid
4. cylinder or cube
5–6. Accept reasonable drawings.
5.
6.
7. 16 ft
8. 55 ft
9. $2\frac{2}{3}$

Page 125
1. 108 cm²
2. 517 m²
3. 360 mm²
4. 228 cm²
5. 486 m²
6. 144 cm²
7. 54 in.²
8. 93 cm²
9. 8 cubes, 12 cubes, 6 cubes, 1 cube

Page 126
1. 706.5 cm², 706.5 cm²
2. 20 cm
3. 94.2 cm
4. 1,884 cm²
5. 3,297cm²
6. 7,536 cm²
7. 527.52 cm²
8. 113.04 m²
9.

Page 127
1. about 1,000 cm²
2. about 13 cm
3. about 20 liters
4. about $16
5. $27
6. $15

Page 127 (cont.)
7. 5 students

Page 128
1. 72 cm²; 864 cm³
2. 78.5 cm²; 628 cm³
3. 90 mm²; 1,620 mm³
4. 6 m³
5. 12,560 cm³
6. 64 in.³
7. 420 ft³
8. 452.16 cm³
9. 18 ft.³
10.
11.

Page 129
1. 100 cm², 400 cm³
2. 28.26 m²; 169.56 m³
3. 28.26 m²; 56.52 m³
4. 452.16 m³
5. 220 cm³
6. 150.72 cm³
7. 36 in.³
8. 1,440 in.³

Page 130
1. 3,000 cm³, 3 kg
2. 6 cm³, 6 g
3. 50 mL, 50 cm³
4. 300mL, 300 g
5. 1,500 cm³, 1.5 kg
6. 2.6 L, 2,600 cm³
7. 9 m³, 9,000 kg
8. 6 L, 6 kg
9. 700 cm³
10. ⁻273°C
11. One possible solution is given.

```
        8
        3
  4 1 7 5 9
        2
        6
```

Page 131
1–6. See page 156 for triangle.
1. 1 6 15 20 15 6 1
2. 1 7 21 35 35 21 7 1
3. 1 8 28 56 70 56 28 8 1
4. 28
5. 15, 21
6. $4^2 + 6 = 16 + 6$
7. 37, 50, 65

Core Skills: Math, Grade 7, Answer Key (cont.)

Page 131 (cont.)

8. 27 $(5^2 + 2)$, 38 $(6^2 + 2)$, 51 $(7^2 + 2)$

Page 132

1. One possible answer is given.

2. Answers will vary.
3. 3 : 4
4. 1 : 4
5. 3 : 1

Mixed Review

1. 53.29 in.²   3. 28.26 in.²
2. 84 cm²   4. 7.28 mm²

Page 133

1.

Set A	Set B
0	2
1	3
2	4
3	5
4	6
5	7

2. $n + 2$
3. ⁻2, ⁻1, 0, 1, 2, 3; ⁻6, ⁻3, 0, 3, 6, 9
4.

5–6. See page 156.
7. Check problem.

Page 134

1. It is tripled.
2. It is $\frac{1}{4}$ of the original area.
3. Divide the height by 2.
4. Divide the height by 6.
5. $A = \frac{5}{2} b$

Page 134 (cont.)

6. It increases 9 times.
7. It increases 12 times.
8. 150 in.³

Mixed Review

1. 169.6 in.²   1. 37.7 m³
2. 856 cm²   2. 83.7 in.³

Page 135

1–2.

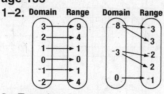

3. Exercise 1
4. Yes; Each element of the domain is matched to exactly one element of the range.
5. No; 5 is matched to more than one element of the range.
6. No; 16 and 9 are each matched to more than one element of the range.
7. Yes; Each element of the domain is matched to exactly one element of the range.
8. 8 units²

Page 136

1–3. See page 156.
1. yes
2. no
3. yes
4. Solutions will vary. $y = 3x - 2$; (0, ⁻2), (1, 1), (2, 4); yes
5. 240%
6. n^2

Page 137

1–3. Check drawings.
1. yes

Page 137 (cont.)

2. no
3. yes
4. no; 7^2, 8^2, 16, 49, 64, 65 ≠ 64
5. yes; 5^2, 12^2, 25, 144, 169, 169 = 169
6. no; 5^2, 9^2, 25, 36, 81, 61 ≠ 81
7. yes; 16^2, 20^2, 144, 256, 400, 400 = 400
8. yes
9. no
10. yes
11. One possible answer: 8 and 6. 36 + 64 = 100 = 4(25). It is a multiple of 25.

Page 138

1. 12.8 in.
2. 21.2 m
3. 13 m
4. 10.8 cm
5. 17 in.
6. no; $15^2 + 15^2 ≠ 20^2$
7. yes; $15^2 + 36^2 = 39^2$
8. $\sqrt{89} ≈ 9.4$ ft
9. 45 sq ft
10. 6 fish
11. 130 ft; 300 ft

Page 139

1. Jennifer is 12; her brother is 8.
2. 4 kilometers
3. ⁻5 and 3
4. 2 and ⁻6
5. yes
6. $12,480
7. Possible answer: Draw a diagram. It helps me to organize the information given and to see what is needed to solve the problem.

Core Skills: Math, Grade 7, Graphics

Page 11

4.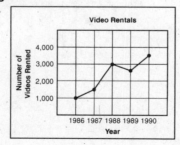

Video Rentals

Page 13

1.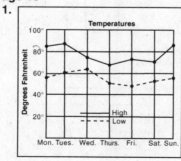

Temperatures

Page 13

4.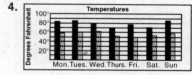

Temperatures

Core Skills: Math, Grade 7, Graphics (cont.)

Page 51

7.

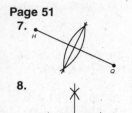

8.

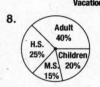

Page 74

6.

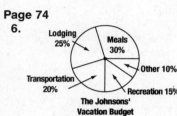

8.

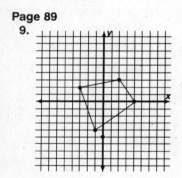

Page 89

9.

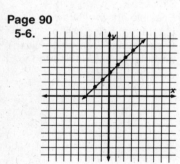

Page 90

5-6.

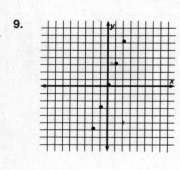

9.

Page 121

5.

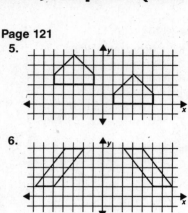

6.

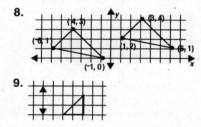

7.

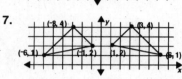

(⁻8, 4)   (3, 4)

(⁻6, 1)   (⁻1, 2)   (1, 2)   (6, 1)

8.

(⁻4, 3)   (3, 4)

(⁻6, 1)   (1, 2)   (6, 1)

(⁻1, 0)

9.

Page 122

5.

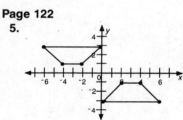

6.

7.

Page 131

1-6.

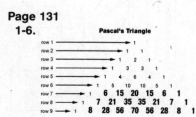

Pascal's Triangle

row 1 → 1
row 2 → 1 1
row 3 → 1 2 1
row 4 → 1 3 3 1
row 5 → 1 4 6 4 1
row 6 → 1 5 10 10 5 1
row 7 → 1 6 15 20 15 6 1
row 8 → 1 7 21 35 35 21 7 1
row 9 → 1 8 28 56 70 56 28 8 1

Page 133

5.

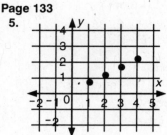

6.

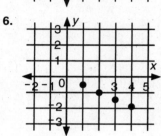

Page 136

1.

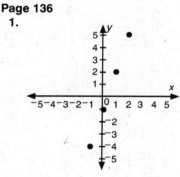

2.

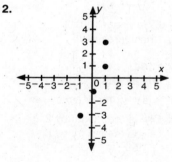

3.

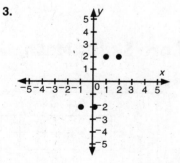